Table of Contents

1 Chapter 1: Introduction to Attribution

Attribution, at its core, is the acknowledgement of origin. It's the intellectual thread that connects a creator to their creation, a fundamental concept underpinning copyright law and intellectual property rights. Think of it as the digital signature, the indelible mark that says, "This is mine, or at least, this came from me." But in the ever-expanding universe of digital production, this simple act of acknowledgement has become increasingly complex, fraught with challenges that demand a more nuanced understanding. We start with the simple view to build up a framework to protect authors from unauthorized use.

The core of authorship hinges on several key elements: originality, intent, and demonstrable contribution. Originality doesn't necessarily mean absolute novelty – the creation of something from nothing. It implies a degree of independent thought, skill, and judgment invested in the work. Intent refers to the conscious desire to create, to express an idea or concept in a tangible form. And demonstrable contribution speaks to the tangible evidence of that intent, the specific actions taken to bring the creation into being. Historically, these elements were relatively straightforward to establish. A painter signed their canvas; a writer put their name on the title page. The physical act of creation provided inherent proof of authorship. This is the foundation that we want to protect, by building some bounds around it.

The digital age, however, has upended these traditional notions. The ease with which digital works can be copied, modified, and redistributed has created a veritable Wild West of content, where attribution can be easily obscured, intentionally or unintentionally. Imagine a photograph shared across social media, stripped of its metadata, endlessly replicated and repurposed without any credit to the original photographer. Or consider a piece of code, copied and pasted into multiple projects, its original author forgotten in the digital shuffle. These are just two small examples of the broader issues that arise as we shift toward an ever growing digital production and collaboration world.

Consider the rise of collaborative projects. These projects are often the result of contributions from multiple individuals, each adding their unique skills and perspectives to the final product. Determining individual contributions can be difficult, leading to disputes over authorship and ownership. We need to clearly define these situations. What percentage of a piece can one change and still give credit to the original author? This is the main question we hope to answer with a series of bounds. The open-source software movement, for example, relies heavily on collaborative development, but the attribution of individual contributions can be a complex and contentious issue. Who gets credit for what? How do we ensure that all contributors are properly acknowledged? How can the authorship of these projects be validated in court?

Then there's the thorny issue of derivative works. How much modification is permissible before a work loses its connection to the original source? What constitutes "fair use" in the digital realm? These are questions that have plagued copyright law for decades, and the ease of digital manipulation has only made them more difficult to answer. Think of a song sampled and remixed by another artist. At what point does the remix become its own distinct work, deserving of its own copyright protection? What level of compensation is due to the original artist? Or what if the song is used as background music in a video game? A series of bounds could help determine where the creator's ownership is being encroached upon, with respect to the original creator.

Furthermore, we must acknowledge the increasing role of machines in the creative process. This presents a unique challenge to traditional notions of authorship. Is a program considered the author of the work it produces? Or is the author the person who designed and programmed the program? The current legal system does not have clearly defined boundaries. As these types of programs become more sophisticated, the lines between human and artificial creation will continue to blur, demanding new legal and ethical frameworks for attribution. This is the issue that will drive the need to develop bounds around proper authorization and derivative use, with the goal of protecting an original author's ownership.

The ease of copying and distributing digital content has also led to a proliferation of plagiarism. Students, researchers, and writers alike face the temptation to cut and paste from online sources without proper attribution. The consequences of plagiarism can be severe, ranging from academic penalties to professional disgrace. But how do we effectively detect and prevent plagiarism in the digital age? How do we educate individuals about the importance of proper attribution? One can think of these bounds as a type of plagiarism detection, which is a tool to protect one's original work.

Finally, the global nature of the internet presents additional challenges to attribution. Copyright laws vary from country to country, and enforcing copyright across international borders can be a complex and expensive undertaking. How do we ensure that authors are properly credited and compensated for their work, regardless of where it is used? How do we navigate the legal and cultural differences that can impact attribution practices? Without some standard, our intellectual property rights are very much at risk.

Navigating this complex landscape requires a multifaceted approach. We need to develop new technologies and tools that can help us track and verify attribution in the digital realm. We need to educate individuals about the importance of proper attribution and the consequences of plagiarism. And we need to work together to create a more equitable and sustainable system for protecting intellectual property rights in the digital age. This is the challenge we are seeking to address, and the bounds we are defining are the first step. We are hoping to create the next step toward clearly defining ownership, but still allowing for use.

1.1 Core Concepts of Authorship

Authorship, at its core, is about claiming and receiving recognition for the creation of something original. It's more than just the act of putting pen to paper, fingers to keyboard, or code to compiler; it's about the unique intellectual contribution that results in a tangible or intangible work. This contribution must be demonstrably original, meaning it can't be a mere reproduction of something that already exists. Think of it as the fingerprint on a piece of art, the signature on a novel, or the commit hash on a piece of software. It's what distinguishes your work from all others and connects it uniquely to you. The concept of originality is often debated, especially when dealing with derivative works or collaborations, but the fundamental principle remains: the author must have contributed something new and unique to the creation.

Originality doesn't necessarily mean inventing something entirely from scratch. It can involve creatively combining existing elements in a novel way, adding a unique perspective, or significantly transforming existing material. Consider a musician who samples existing songs to create a new composition. The originality lies not in the samples themselves, but in the way they are arranged, combined, and transformed to create something new and distinct. Similarly, a writer might draw inspiration from historical events but create a fictional narrative that offers a fresh interpretation or explores new themes. The key is that the author must demonstrably add their own creative stamp to the work, making it something more than just a copy or slight variation of something that already exists. We need to focus on the intellectual work that is required in the process of being an author.

Intellectual contribution goes beyond mere physical effort. It involves the cognitive processes of conception, design, and execution. This means that the author must have actively participated in the creation of the work, contributing their ideas, skills, and expertise. Consider a software developer who contributes code to an open-source project. Their intellectual contribution lies not only in writing the code itself but also in designing the algorithms, debugging the errors, and testing the functionality. Similarly, an architect's intellectual contribution lies not only in drawing the blueprints but also in conceiving the overall design, selecting the materials, and ensuring the structural integrity of the building.

The definition of an "author" can vary depending on the context. In copyright law, the author is typically defined as the person who created the work. However, in collaborative projects, determining authorship can be more complex. Is it the person who had the initial idea? The person who wrote the majority of the text? The person who provided the funding? Or all of them? The answer often depends on the specific agreements and understandings between the parties involved.

In some cases, authorship may be shared equally among all contributors. In others, it may be attributed primarily to the person who made the most significant intellectual contribution. The definition should always be well defined.
Now, let's not forget the role of technology in shaping our understanding of authorship. Digital tools have made it easier than ever to create, copy, and share content. This has led to new challenges in attributing authorship and protecting intellectual property. For example, what happens when a work is created using AI tools? Is the AI the author? Or is it the person who prompted the AI and curated the results? These are complex questions that require careful consideration and new legal frameworks.
Think about the use of generative models for writing text. While the model might produce grammatically correct and even stylistically impressive text, it's essentially regurgitating patterns and information it has learned from the vast amounts of data it was trained on. It lacks the intentionality, the lived experience, and the unique perspective that a human author brings to their work. Therefore, while an AI might be a useful tool for assisting authors, it shouldn't be considered an author in its own right. The human author is still responsible for the overall concept, the selection of prompts, the editing and refining of the output, and the ultimate message that the work conveys.
Attribution is, therefore, the act of acknowledging and giving credit to the rightful author of a work. It's a fundamental principle of academic integrity, ethical publishing, and respect for

intellectual property. Proper attribution ensures that authors receive the recognition they deserve for their creative efforts and prevents others from taking credit for their work. It also allows readers to trace the origins of ideas and build upon existing knowledge. It is important, to prevent any kind of plagiarism.

How does one properly attribute authorship? There are various methods, depending on the context. In academic writing, citations and bibliographies are used to give credit to the sources of information and ideas. In creative works, such as books and films, credit is typically given in the form of author names, copyright notices, and acknowledgments. In software development, code repositories and licensing agreements are used to track contributions and protect intellectual property. It's crucial to use the appropriate attribution method for the specific type of work and to ensure that all sources are properly acknowledged.

The act of attributing authorship is not merely a formality; it's an ethical imperative. It upholds the principles of honesty, fairness, and respect for intellectual property. Failure to attribute authorship can have serious consequences, ranging from academic sanctions to legal penalties. Plagiarism, for example, is a form of academic dishonesty that involves presenting someone else's work as your own. It can result in failing grades, expulsion from school, and damage to your reputation. Copyright infringement is a legal violation that involves using someone else's copyrighted work without permission. It can result in fines, lawsuits, and even criminal

charges. It is an important rule.
Ultimately, understanding the core concepts of authorship is essential for navigating the complexities of the digital age. As creators, we must strive to produce original and intellectually stimulating work, and we must be diligent in giving credit to the sources of our inspiration. As consumers of content, we must be critical of the information we encounter and demand that authors be properly attributed. By upholding the principles of authorship, we can foster a culture of creativity, innovation, and respect for intellectual property. Doing so we will safeguard the bounds of Authors' Production.

1.2 The Landscape of Digital Production

The digital realm has fundamentally reshaped how content is created, disseminated, and consumed. It's a dynamic ecosystem, brimming with both unprecedented opportunities and thorny challenges for authors seeking to protect their intellectual property. For a beginner venturing into this space, grasping the key features is paramount to navigating safely and effectively. Today, the landscape consists of digital works such as images, videos, texts, code and designs. This shift has led to an increase in different forms of digital content creation, from individual bloggers sharing opinions to large corporations developing complex software programs. Authors must be aware of the technological frameworks involved in order to navigate safely and effectively. The technology stack and software are the basis of creation and the distribution channels are just as important, if not more, in the modern digital ecosystem.

Understanding content creation tools is essential. No longer is authorship confined to pen and paper or even the traditional word processor. We now have advanced image editing software, video editing suites, music production tools, and coding environments that empower individuals with capabilities previously reserved for large organizations. A budding author should familiarize themselves with the available tools, selecting those that best suit their chosen medium and creative style. Furthermore, many of these tools now incorporate elements that assist in the documentation of provenance and authorship, so it is important to understand what information you can imbue within your work that makes attribution later easier.

Distribution channels have undergone a similarly dramatic transformation. Instead of relying solely on traditional publishers or distributors, authors can leverage social media platforms, online marketplaces, streaming services, and personal websites to reach their audiences directly. Understanding the nuances of each platform – its audience demographics, content formats, and algorithms – is vital for maximizing reach and impact. Platforms such as YouTube and Vimeo have created a surge in the number of online video creators. Similarly, the advent of music streaming services has transformed how artists distribute their work and get paid.

Then there is copyright. Protecting your work in the digital realm requires a proactive approach to copyright. This involves understanding copyright law, registering your works when applicable, and utilizing digital rights management (DRM) technologies to prevent unauthorized copying and distribution. It's crucial to remember that copyright protection typically begins automatically upon creation of an original work, but formal registration can provide added legal benefits. Moreover, it's not just about protecting against outright theft; it's also about controlling how your work is used and adapted by others, which is where the concept of attribution bounds becomes particularly relevant. The rise of digital rights management (DRM) systems, while controversial, demonstrates efforts to control distribution.

Fair use and transformative works are concepts that are essential for authors who are starting to develop a grasp of copyright law. It is important to understand how the law permits limited use of copyrighted material without permission from the copyright holder. This typically includes commentary, criticism, education and parody. The key factor is whether the new work is "transformative" \item that is, whether it adds something new with a further purpose or different character, and does not substitute for the original use of the work. Navigating this concept requires careful judgment and, in some cases, legal advice. The legal precedents about transformative use are essential for understanding the limits of content creation.

The digital landscape is also rife with collaborative works. Open-source software, jointly written articles, and other content are becoming increasingly common. When authorship is shared, there needs to be a clear and upfront agreement on how ownership and attribution will be handled. This should be done through written contracts that delineate the rights and responsibilities of each contributor, minimizing the potential for disputes down the line. These agreements should define the scope of each contributor's input, the ownership of the final product, and how attribution will be managed.

Watermarking and metadata embedding are two important techniques for providing visibility and credibility of digital assets. Watermarking involves embedding a subtle identifying mark into your digital content, making it difficult to remove without damaging the original work. Metadata embedding involves adding information about authorship, copyright, and usage rights directly into the file itself. These techniques are not foolproof, but they can act as deterrents and provide evidence of ownership in case of infringement. Services such as Digimarc can be used for a professional approach.

The landscape has new challenges. With increasing interconnectedness comes greater risk of plagiarism and copyright infringement. Monitoring the internet for unauthorized uses of your work is crucial, but can also be overwhelming. Consider using tools designed to detect copyright infringement, and be prepared to take legal action when necessary. Copyright infringement detection services, for instance, scan the web for unauthorized copies of your work, alerting you to potential violations.

The digital realm is a global stage, and authors must be cognizant of international copyright laws. Copyright laws vary from country to country, so understanding the laws applicable in the jurisdictions where your work is likely to be accessed is essential. International treaties, such as the Berne Convention, provide some degree of harmonization, but local nuances can still be significant. The World Intellectual Property Organization (WIPO) plays a key role in harmonizing international IP laws.

Looking ahead, the digital production will certainly continue to evolve at a rapid pace. New technologies, such as blockchain and decentralized platforms, are emerging that could revolutionize how authorship is managed and protected. These technologies offer the potential to create more transparent and secure systems for tracking provenance and enforcing copyright. As an author, it's important to stay abreast of these developments and be prepared to adapt your strategies accordingly. Decentralized platforms are being developed to give creators greater control over their content.

Ultimately, navigating the digital landscape requires a multifaceted approach that combines legal knowledge, technological savvy, and proactive monitoring. By understanding the key features of this ecosystem, authors can effectively protect their work, assert their rights, and thrive in the digital age. Remaining informed, flexible, and proactive is key to mastering the digital landscape and fostering a successful career as an author. This involves continuous learning, adaptation to new technologies, and engagement with the legal and ethical issues surrounding digital authorship.

2 Chapter 2: Fundamental Bound Frameworks

Attribution bounds, in their most fundamental form, serve as the foundational pillars upon which more complex attribution systems are built. They represent a predefined range, a sort of 'safe zone,' that delineates the permissible extent of modification or utilization of an author's work before it infringes upon their attribution rights. These bounds can be visualized as fences, marking the legal and ethical boundaries within which others can freely interact with a copyrighted creation. Establishing clear and defensible bounds is essential to protect creators from misappropriation, while also allowing for innovation and the creation of derivative works. Without these guideposts, navigating the landscape of intellectual property becomes a treacherous endeavor, fraught with uncertainty and potential litigation.

The very definition of a bound in this context hinges on several key properties. First and foremost is clarity: a bound must be expressed in a manner that is easily understood and applied. Ambiguity renders a bound useless, as it leaves room for interpretation and exploitation. Secondly, enforceability is paramount; a bound must be capable of being practically implemented and monitored. A theoretical bound that cannot be translated into real-world action is ultimately ineffective. Thirdly, reasonableness plays a vital role; a bound that is excessively restrictive can stifle creativity and hinder progress, while one that is too lenient offers inadequate protection. Finally, context-sensitivity must be considered; a bound that works well in one situation may be completely inappropriate in another. The nature of the work, the intended use, and the relevant legal frameworks all play a role in determining the appropriate scope of an attribution bound. These properties ensure that the established boundaries are fair, effective, and adaptable to diverse situations.

Moving beyond the general definition, let's consider different types of attribution bounds. A simple, yet commonly used, form is the percentage-based bound. This type of bound limits the amount of an author's work that can be used in a derivative creation. For example, a bound might specify that no more than 10% of an original musical composition can be incorporated into a new song without proper attribution and permission. Another type is the modification bound, which focuses on the degree to which an author's work can be altered. This bound might stipulate that any modification that significantly alters the original meaning or intent of a work requires explicit consent from the author. Then there's the purpose-based bound, which restricts the use of an author's work to a specific purpose or context. For instance, a photograph licensed for editorial use cannot be used for commercial advertising without violating the attribution bound. Finally, we have combinational bounds, these blends elements from multiple categories to construct a more precise delineation. As an example, a combinational bound could stipulate that a maximum of 5% of an original text can be utilized, but only if it's significantly altered and not used for commercial purposes. Each bound type offers a distinctive method for securing authors' rights by setting precise limits on how their creations can be employed.

While simple bounds offer an initial layer of protection, they are not without their limitations. One of the primary challenges is their inherent oversimplification. Digital content, especially creative works, often exhibit complex and nuanced relationships that cannot be adequately captured by simple percentage or modification rules. Imagine a musical sample lasting only a few seconds that forms the core hook of a popular song, a simple percentage based attribution would deem this use fair due to its insignificant size. Another significant limitation stems from their inflexibility. As mentioned earlier, the appropriateness of an attribution bound is highly context-dependent. Simple bounds typically fail to account for the specific circumstances of each case, leading to potentially unfair or ineffective outcomes. Moreover, simple bounds can be easily circumvented. Individuals seeking to exploit an author's work can often find ways to technically comply with the letter of the bound while still violating its spirit. For example, someone could slightly alter a copyrighted image just enough to fall outside the bounds of a modification rule, while still essentially copying the original work. The reality is that these simple rules do not consider the intent of the parties using the copyrighted material. Because of these challenges, there's a clear need for more sophisticated and adaptable attribution bounds that can effectively address the complexities of modern digital content creation. The next steps involve creating bounds which involve more precise models.

Looking ahead, the inadequacies of basic bounds highlight the necessity for advanced frameworks capable of managing the subtleties inherent in digital authorship. Statistical bounds offer a promising avenue, incorporating probabilities and data-driven insights to more accurately establish attribution. Causal inference models push further, aiming to discern causal relationships between original works and derivative creations, thus giving a deeper awareness of authorial impact. Information-theoretic bounds, meanwhile, employ principles of entropy and mutual information to assess attribution uncertainty, providing a quantitative benchmark for permitted use. By embracing these advanced methods, we can craft attribution frameworks that are both more precise and more equitable, reinforcing the rights of creators in a dynamic digital environment. These bounds help provide more than just legal parameters, they can help bring fairness and allow for flexibility when needed.

2.1 Bound Definition and Properties

The very essence of an attribution bound hinges on its definition: a quantifiable limit that delineates acceptable usage or modification of an authored work without infringing upon the original author's rights. This isn't merely a vague guideline, but a precisely defined mathematical or logical constraint. Imagine a sculptor creating a marble statue; an attribution bound might specify the maximum percentage of the original sculpture that can be altered before it's considered a new, distinct work, or perhaps even define specific elements of the statue that must remain unchanged to maintain the original artist's attribution. This bound provides clarity, transforming subjective judgments into objective measurements. The concept isn't limited to physical art, either. Consider software code: an attribution bound could dictate the minimum percentage of original code that must be present in a derivative work, or require clear attribution of the original author in the software's documentation. Defining these boundaries necessitates a deep understanding of both the original work and the changes made to it, requiring careful analysis and quantification. Therefore, a robust definition of an attribution bound is paramount, not just for legal clarity, but also for fostering creativity by setting clear parameters within which derivative works can flourish.

Crucially, attribution bounds aren't arbitrary numbers plucked from thin air; they possess inherent properties that dictate their utility and validity. One fundamental property is measurability. An attribution bound must be expressible in quantifiable terms – whether it's a percentage, a ratio, or a more complex metric based on information theory or statistical analysis. Without measurability, the bound remains ambiguous and unenforceable. Another essential property is specificity. A well-defined attribution bound targets particular aspects of the work. For example, it could be the number of original lines remaining in a text, or perhaps the key musical motifs preserved in a song. A non-specific bound, such as "significant alterations," is open to subjective interpretation and thus weakened. Further, enforceability is key: A bound is useless if it cannot be applied in a real-world context. This means the criteria for assessing the bound must be clear and objective, not requiring interpretive leaps that may be too subjective for a court to agree upon. This demands that bounds are based on evidence, whether direct or statistical, and that they avoid value judgements of creativity. In fact, good bounds should ideally be applicable using computational tools to automate the process of detection.

Expanding on this concept, it's important to recognize the property of context-dependence. The appropriate attribution bound will change drastically depending on the type of work, the specific usage scenario, and the prevailing legal framework. A stricter bound may be necessary for commercial use compared to non-commercial parody, for instance. Imagine sampling a drum beat from a song; the permissible alteration and usage might differ vastly depending on whether it's for a small indie project or a major pop album. The legal framework shapes bounds through laws governing fair use, copyright, and intellectual property. Thus, attribution bounds must be tailored to the specific context to remain relevant and effective. Finally, and perhaps the most subtle property of all, is that of adaptability. The digital landscape is constantly evolving, with new forms of creative expression emerging all the time. Attribution bounds must be flexible enough to adapt to these changes. Fixed, rigid bounds may quickly become obsolete as new technologies and artistic practices push the boundaries of authorship. This means bounds must be regularly re-evaluated and adjusted to remain relevant in a dynamic environment.

Beyond these core properties, attribution bounds can be further characterized by their granularity. A fine-grained bound might focus on individual elements within a work, such as specific characters in a novel or individual melodies in a musical piece. A coarse-grained bound, on the other hand, might consider the overall structure or style of the work. The appropriate level of granularity depends on the specific goals of the attribution analysis. Consider the example of a film adaptation of a novel. A fine-grained bound might examine the fidelity of individual scenes or lines of dialogue, while a coarse-grained bound might focus on the overall narrative structure and thematic elements. The choice of granularity can significantly impact the outcome of the attribution assessment. Additionally, one should always consider the degree of interpretability. How easily can a regular person, not a legal or technical expert, understand what the bound is attempting to assess, and why? Bounds should be designed to be interpretable to facilitate collaboration between experts and to increase public understanding of intellectual property issues. Delving further, attribution bounds exhibit the characteristic of monotonicity. This implies that as the degree of modification or incorporation increases, the strength of the attribution claim by the original author generally decreases. Think of a remix of a song: the more the original track is altered and new elements are added, the weaker the claim that the remix is solely attributable to the original artist. This isn't always a linear relationship, and there might be thresholds where attribution shifts abruptly. However, monotonicity provides a general guideline for understanding how attribution changes with the extent of modification. Monotonicity should also be considered in the context of iterative bounds. Some creative workflows involve layers of modification. A photograph might be digitally manipulated, then incorporated into a larger digital artwork, which in turn is printed and physically altered. Bounds for each of these stages might be independent, but the cumulative effect of all these changes must also be considered. In such scenarios, the iterative nature of the bounds becomes a crucial property to consider.

The concept of resilience of attribution bounds, meaning that a small perturbation of data shall not lead to large modification of the bound value. It should allow for reasonable variations in the data without causing drastic changes in the assessed attribution. For example, consider the case of image recognition. If an image of a famous painting is subjected to minor noise or compression artifacts, an effective attribution bound should still be able to recognize the artwork and not be overly sensitive to these small variations.

Importantly, attribution bounds are not infallible. They can have limitations. Simple rule-based bounds, for instance, may struggle to capture the nuances of creative expression. Statistical bounds rely on data, and can be skewed by biases or incomplete datasets. Information theoretic bounds can be computationally expensive. Understanding these limitations is crucial for interpreting the results of attribution analyses and avoiding over-reliance on any single type of bound. When simple bounds fall short, it may be necessary to combine multiple types of bounds, or to incorporate expert human judgment.

Finally, we need to consider the ethical dimensions of attribution bounds. The goal is not just to protect authors' rights, but also to promote innovation and creativity. Overly strict bounds can stifle derivative works and limit artistic expression. It is important to strike a balance between protecting authors and encouraging new forms of creative expression, especially in collaborative works. Finding this balance requires careful consideration of the social and cultural context in which the attribution bounds are applied. Attribution bound values must align with principles of fairness and equity to ensure that the rights of all stakeholders are respected.

2.2 Types of Attribution Bounds

Attribution bounds are not monolithic; they exist along a spectrum, each suited to different contexts and offering varying degrees of protection. Understanding these types is crucial for selecting the most appropriate framework for a given situation. Let's first examine the fundamental distinction between static and dynamic bounds. Static bounds define a fixed threshold, often expressed as a percentage or a specific set of alterations, beyond which a work is considered a derivative requiring proper attribution. Imagine a scenario where a digital image is altered. A static bound might dictate that any modification exceeding 20% of the original image's pixels necessitates attribution. While simple to implement, static bounds often fail to capture the nuances of creative contribution. A minor, yet transformative, change might be missed, while insignificant alterations could trigger unnecessary attribution.

Dynamic bounds, on the other hand, adapt to the specific characteristics of the work in question. They consider factors such as the originality, complexity, and creative investment involved in the original piece. For instance, a highly original and complex artwork might warrant a stricter dynamic bound, requiring attribution even for relatively minor alterations that significantly impact its aesthetic value or underlying message. These types of bounds often rely on more sophisticated analytical techniques, like comparing the frequency of certain keywords or musical notes between the original and derived work, or even going as far as judging if the alterations have been trivial or game-changing. However, dynamic bounds can be more complex to implement and require a deeper understanding of the creative work itself, as well as more computational power. The subjective nature of assessing "creative investment" can also introduce bias and inconsistency, so these are better used by experts in the matter.

Then, let's delve into what we can call similarity-based and feature-based bounds. Similarity-based bounds hinge on measuring the overall similarity between two works. This might involve calculating the edit distance between two texts, or comparing the color palettes and compositional elements of two images. A high degree of similarity would suggest a need for attribution. One common approach here is the use of cosine similarity, where we measure the angle between the vector representations of two documents. The smaller the angle, the greater the similarity. However, similarity alone can be misleading. Two works might be highly similar due to shared influences or common source material, rather than direct copying. Therefore, similarity-based bounds must be used with caution, particularly when dealing with genres or fields where derivative works are common, or the original author has used common information.

Feature-based bounds, in contrast, focus on identifying specific features that have been copied or derived from the original work. These features might include unique melodies, distinctive writing styles, or specific design elements. The presence of these features in a derivative work would trigger the need for attribution. This approach is particularly useful for detecting plagiarism, where subtle but identifiable features of the original work are reproduced in a new context. For example, identifying the reuse of a specific algorithm in a software program, or the presence of a unique poetic meter in a derivative poem. Feature-based bounds can be more robust than similarity-based bounds, as they are less susceptible to being fooled by superficial similarities. Still, they require careful selection of features and may miss instances of transformative adaptation where the original features are significantly altered.

Another critical distinction lies between quantitative and qualitative bounds. Quantitative bounds rely on measurable metrics and numerical thresholds. These metrics could include the percentage of code copied, the number of words plagiarized, or the degree of color alteration. A quantitative bound might state that any reuse of more than 10% of the original code requires attribution. These types of bounds offer objectivity and ease of enforcement, but often fail to capture the qualitative aspects of authorship. A small amount of code, if it represents a critical innovation or core functionality, might warrant attribution even if it falls below the quantitative threshold. Similarly, copying a small number of highly original and impactful phrases might be more significant than copying a larger number of generic sentences.

Qualitative bounds, on the other hand, consider the subjective and artistic aspects of authorship. They assess the originality, creativity, and impact of the copied or derived material. A qualitative bound might require attribution if the derived work significantly diminishes the value or reputation of the original work, or if it appropriates the core message or artistic vision. These types of bounds are inherently more subjective and require expert judgment to apply. They are often used in cases involving artistic works, where the qualitative impact of copying is more important than the quantitative amount. This subjectivity is, of course, a vulnerability, making them more open to legal challenges and requiring a panel of subject matter experts to come to a judgment.

Finally, we should address explicit and implicit bounds. Explicit bounds are formally defined and publicly declared. These might be set by copyright law, licensing agreements, or institutional policies. An explicit bound might state that any commercial use of a creative work requires attribution and payment of royalties. These types of bounds provide clarity and predictability, but can be inflexible and may not adapt well to evolving creative practices. Furthermore, they are subject to legal interpretation and may be challenged in court.

Implicit bounds, on the other hand, are based on social norms, ethical considerations, and professional standards. They are not formally defined, but are widely understood and accepted within a particular community or field. An implicit bound might dictate that scholars should always cite their sources, even when the ideas are widely known or have been rephrased. These types of bounds promote ethical behavior and foster a culture of respect for authorship. However, they are often ambiguous and can vary across different communities or cultures. They are also difficult to enforce, relying primarily on social pressure and professional reputation. As one can see, the selection and application of attribution bounds is not a simple task. It requires careful consideration of the context, the type of work, and the desired level of protection. A combination of different types of bounds may be necessary to create a comprehensive and effective attribution framework.

2.3 Limitations of Simple Bounds

Attribution bounds, especially when constructed using simple rules or metrics, offer an initial layer of protection and clarity, yet they inherently possess limitations that can lead to both under-protection and over-restriction of authors' rights. We have to start by acknowledging that a single metric, such as the percentage of verbatim copying, rarely captures the full nuance of intellectual contribution. To be fair, such simplicity might seem appealing for its ease of implementation and understanding, particularly in preliminary assessments or when dealing with a high volume of potential infringements. Imagine a scenario where a piece of software is flagged as potentially infringing because 20% of its code is identical to a copyrighted library. A simple bound might automatically trigger an investigation. The problem arises when that 20% comprises fundamental algorithms or standard programming practices that are virtually indispensable for any program of that type. Here, a rigid, simple bound would unfairly flag a legitimate use as infringement.

On the other hand, simple bounds can also fail to adequately protect the author's intellectual property when derivative works cleverly circumvent the defined limitations. For example, a simple rule might state that altering more than 30% of the original work constitutes a "transformative" use, thereby falling outside the scope of infringement. However, someone could intentionally alter 31% of a text by replacing synonyms or rearranging sentences, effectively paraphrasing the original work while retaining its core ideas, structure, and expressive qualities. In this case, the derivative work has exploited the simplicity of the bound to misappropriate the original author's intellectual creation, despite technically complying with the alteration threshold. Another real-world instance can come from the world of music. Imagine a song with a very distinctive melody and chord progression. A simple bound focused solely on note-for-note copying would be easily circumvented by slightly altering the rhythm or tempo, yet the derivative song would still be instantly recognizable and commercially benefiting from the original composer's creativity.

One critical shortcoming of simple bounds lies in their inability to account for the qualitative aspects of authorship. They often treat all elements of a work as equally important, overlooking the fact that certain sections, characters, or even specific phrases may carry a disproportionate amount of the author's creative contribution. Consider a novel where the plot is generic, but the characters are highly original and well-developed. A simple bound focusing on plot similarity would fail to recognize the significant intellectual property vested in the characters. Similarly, in a visual artwork, the unique style or brushstrokes might be more important than the overall composition. A simple bound based on color palette or geometric arrangement would not capture the essence of the artist's unique expression.

Further complicating matters is the problem of contextual dependence. The same level of similarity might be permissible in one context but infringing in another. For instance, quoting a few lines from a poem in a scholarly critique is generally considered fair use, while using the same lines in a commercial advertisement would likely be seen as infringement. Similarly, the reuse of factual information is typically allowed, even if expressed in similar language, whereas the wholesale copying of creative expression is not. Simple bounds often lack the sophistication to distinguish between these nuanced scenarios, leading to inconsistent and potentially unjust outcomes.

Addressing the limitations of simple attribution bounds requires moving towards more sophisticated, context-aware frameworks. This includes incorporating statistical models that can assess the probability of authorship based on multiple features, as well as causal inference techniques that can identify the impact of specific changes on the overall attribution. Information-theoretic approaches can also provide valuable insights into the degree of originality and transformation achieved in derivative works. Ultimately, the goal is to develop bounds that are both rigorous and flexible, capable of adapting to the diverse and evolving landscape of digital content creation. This is not to say that simple bounds are entirely without value. They can serve as a useful starting point for identifying potential infringements and can be particularly helpful in situations where speed and efficiency are paramount. However, it is crucial to recognize their limitations and to supplement them with more advanced techniques when necessary. They also provide a basis from which more complex systems can be built. Starting with clearly defined simple bounds allows for the progressive integration of more nuanced factors, such as the originality of particular elements or the context of use, thereby creating a tiered system where simple bounds act as initial filters, and more sophisticated analyses are triggered for cases that require deeper scrutiny.

Another area where simple bounds falter is in dealing with collaborative works. Determining the individual contributions of multiple authors can be incredibly challenging, especially in creative endeavors where ideas are fluid and contributions are intertwined. A simple bound might assign equal weight to all contributors, overlooking the fact that some may have played a more pivotal role in shaping the final product. Additionally, simple bounds typically struggle to address the issue of de minimis copying, where small amounts of copyrighted material are used without permission. While such uses may seem insignificant on the surface, they can still infringe on the author's rights, particularly if they are repeated across multiple works. Similarly, simple bounds may fail to account for the cumulative effect of multiple minor infringements, which, taken together, can significantly harm the author's commercial interests.

Therefore, relying solely on simple bounds can create a false sense of security, both for authors and for those who create derivative works. Authors may underestimate the extent to which their work is being misappropriated, while creators of derivative works may overestimate the degree to which they are protected from infringement claims. This can lead to legal disputes, financial losses, and a chilling effect on creativity. The future of attribution bounds lies in developing frameworks that are more nuanced, adaptable, and comprehensive. This requires incorporating a wide range of factors, including statistical analysis, causal inference, information theory, and expert judgment. It also requires a willingness to move beyond simplistic rules and embrace a more holistic approach to assessing authorship and infringement.

3 Chapter 3: Statistical Attribution Bounds

Statistical Attribution Bounds

To progress beyond simple rules and into the realm of nuanced attribution analysis, we must embrace the power of statistical methods. These methods enable us to quantify uncertainty, model complex relationships, and establish defensible bounds on authorship, especially in cases where the lines of originality become blurred. Our goal is to transform subjective assessments into evidence-based conclusions.

Probabilistic attribution models are the cornerstone of this approach. They allow us to represent the likelihood that a particular author contributed to a given work, considering factors such as stylistic similarity, topical overlap, and source code provenance. Imagine you're analyzing a piece of software. A probabilistic model might consider the frequency of specific coding patterns, variable names, and commenting styles that are characteristic of different developers. The output of the model isn't a definitive "yes" or "no" but rather a probability distribution indicating the likelihood each developer contributed to specific sections of the code. These models often rely on techniques like Markov chains, hidden Markov models, or Bayesian networks to capture the sequential or hierarchical nature of authorship. By modeling these underlying processes, we gain a more robust and accurate understanding of attribution compared to simple similarity metrics.

Now, consider Bayesian attribution bounds. Bayesian statistics provides a natural framework for incorporating prior knowledge about authorship. Let's say we are examining a song with several verses that sound strikingly similar to an existing song. We can use Bayesian methods to incorporate our prior belief about the probability that the verse was copied. This prior might be based on factors like the reputation of the alleged copier, the known history of plagiarism cases involving similar artists, or the overall prevalence of plagiarism in the genre. The beauty of the Bayesian approach lies in its ability to update our beliefs in light of new evidence. As we analyze the music, comparing the verse's melody, harmony, and lyrics to other works, we continuously refine our initial assessment, ultimately arriving at a posterior distribution that reflects our best estimate of authorship given all available data. This posterior distribution can then be used to establish an attribution bound, which might take the form of a credible interval indicating the range of likely contribution percentages from the original author, given a pre-set credibility of e.g. 95%.

Another critical aspect is statistical significance testing. Even with sophisticated probabilistic models, we need to determine whether observed similarities between works are statistically significant or merely due to chance. A simple comparison of word frequencies in two documents might reveal some overlap, but is that overlap enough to conclude that one document infringes upon the copyright of the other? This is where hypothesis testing comes in. We can formulate a null hypothesis that assumes the two documents are independent and then calculate the probability of observing the observed level of similarity if the null hypothesis were true. If this probability (the p-value) is below a pre-defined significance level (e.g., 0.05), we reject the null hypothesis and conclude that there is statistically significant evidence to support the claim of authorship infringement. However, it's crucial to choose the appropriate statistical test for the type of data being analyzed and to control for factors that could inflate the false positive rate.

Addressing data scarcity is always a challenge. In many attribution scenarios, we simply don't have enough data to train robust statistical models. This is especially true when dealing with emerging artistic styles, novel software codebases, or complex multimedia projects. In these cases, we need to employ techniques like transfer learning, where we leverage knowledge gained from analyzing related datasets to improve the performance of our models in data-scarce environments. For example, if we are trying to determine the authorship of a new piece of music, we might use a model trained on a larger dataset of music from the same genre to extract relevant features and inform our attribution analysis. Another approach is to use semi-supervised learning, where we combine labeled

data (e.g., known works by specific authors) with unlabeled data (e.g., potentially infringing works) to improve the accuracy of our models. The key is to carefully select and validate the auxiliary data to ensure that it is relevant to the task at hand and doesn't introduce bias into our analysis.
Finally, we cannot ignore the computational challenges. Applying sophisticated statistical models to large datasets can be computationally intensive, requiring significant processing power and memory. When analyzing large software repositories, complex musical compositions, or high-resolution images, the computational cost of calculating attribution bounds can quickly become prohibitive. To address this, we need to explore techniques like dimensionality reduction, which reduces the number of variables in our models without sacrificing accuracy. Principal component analysis (PCA) and autoencoders are commonly used for this purpose. Another approach is to parallelize our computations, distributing the workload across multiple processors or machines. Cloud computing platforms provide a convenient and cost-effective way to access the computational resources needed to perform large-scale attribution analysis. We must carefully optimize our algorithms and data structures to ensure that our attribution bounds can be calculated efficiently and reliably.

3.1 Probabilistic Attribution Models

Probabilistic attribution models offer a powerful framework for quantifying the likelihood that a particular source or author contributed to a given work. Unlike simpler models that rely on deterministic rules or heuristic measures, probabilistic models embrace uncertainty and provide a nuanced understanding of attribution. These models are particularly useful in complex scenarios where multiple sources may have influenced the final product, or where the exact nature of the contribution is unclear. The core idea is to assign probabilities to different attribution hypotheses, reflecting the degree of belief in each possibility based on available evidence. This approach allows us to move beyond simple binary judgments of "attributed" or "not attributed" and instead provide a more informative assessment of the strength of the attribution claim. To begin, consider a scenario where we are analyzing a piece of text and wish to determine the extent to which it was influenced by different prior publications. A probabilistic model would assign probabilities to each publication, indicating the likelihood that it served as a source for the text in question. These probabilities can be based on a variety of factors, such as the similarity in vocabulary, the presence of shared phrases, and the overall thematic content. The model would then combine these factors to produce an overall attribution score for each potential source.

Constructing a probabilistic attribution model involves several key steps. First, we must define the set of possible sources or authors that could have contributed to the work in question. This could be a list of prior publications, a collection of online documents, or even a set of individual authors. Next, we need to identify the features of the work that are relevant for attribution. These features might include the presence of specific words or phrases, the frequency of certain topics, the style of writing, or the overall structure of the work. For example, in the case of text attribution, we might consider the frequency of different words or the presence of specific n-grams (sequences of n words). Once we have identified the relevant features, we need to quantify the similarity between the work in question and each potential source. This can be done using a variety of techniques, such as cosine similarity, Jaccard index, or edit distance. Each of these techniques provides a measure of the overlap between the features of the two works. However, similarity alone is not sufficient for attribution. We also need to consider the rarity of the shared features. A feature that is common in many different sources is less indicative of attribution than a feature that is rare and specific to a particular source. To account for this, we can use measures such as inverse document frequency (IDF) or term frequency-inverse document frequency (TF-IDF) to weight the features based on their rarity. Finally, we need to combine the similarity scores and rarity weights to produce an overall attribution score for each potential source. This can be done using a variety of techniques, such as a weighted sum or a Bayesian model. The choice of technique will depend on the specific characteristics of the data and the desired properties of the model. Once the model is constructed, it can be used to assign probabilities to different attribution hypotheses. These probabilities can be used to rank the potential sources and to provide a measure of the uncertainty associated with each attribution claim.

Let's delve into the nuances of incorporating Bayesian methods within probabilistic attribution. The Bayesian approach provides a natural way to incorporate prior knowledge and update our beliefs as new evidence becomes available. In this framework, we start with a prior probability distribution over the possible sources or authors. This prior distribution reflects our initial beliefs about the likelihood of each source being the true author. For example, if we know that a particular author is known for writing on a specific topic, we might assign a higher prior probability to that author for a work on the same topic. As we observe the features of the work in question, we can update our prior beliefs using Bayes' theorem. Bayes' theorem tells us how to calculate the posterior probability of each source, given the observed evidence. The posterior probability is proportional to the product of the prior probability and the likelihood of the evidence, given the source. The likelihood of the evidence reflects how well the features of the work match the characteristics of each potential source. For instance, the likelihood might be high for a source that shares many of the same keywords as the work in question. By combining the prior probability and the likelihood, Bayes' theorem allows us to arrive at a more informed assessment of the attribution probabilities. One of the key advantages of the Bayesian approach is its ability to handle uncertainty. The posterior probabilities provide a measure of the uncertainty associated with each attribution claim. This is particularly useful in situations where the evidence is ambiguous or incomplete.

Now, addressing a persistent challenge in attribution: data

scarcity. Often, we face the problem of having limited data available to train our probabilistic models. This can lead to inaccurate attribution probabilities and unreliable results. One approach to mitigating data scarcity is to leverage external knowledge sources. These sources might include large text corpora, knowledge graphs, or expert opinions. For example, we can use a large text corpus to estimate the frequency of different words and phrases. This information can be used to improve the accuracy of our feature weighting schemes. Similarly, we can use a knowledge graph to identify relationships between different concepts. This can help us to identify potential sources that are thematically related to the work in question, even if they do not share many of the same keywords. Another approach to addressing data scarcity is to use transfer learning techniques. Transfer learning involves training a model on a large dataset of related tasks and then adapting the model to the specific attribution task at hand. For example, we can train a model to identify authorship style on a large dataset of published articles and then adapt the model to attribute a specific blog post. By leveraging the knowledge gained from the larger dataset, we can improve the accuracy of our attribution model, even with limited data for the specific task. In essence, you want to use all the potential pieces of information available to you.

Let's consider the computational challenges associated with probabilistic attribution models, especially when dealing with large datasets or complex models. One of the main challenges is the computational cost of calculating the similarity scores between the work in question and all potential sources. This can be particularly time-consuming if the number of sources is large or if the similarity measure is computationally intensive. To address this challenge, we can use techniques such as indexing and hashing to speed up the search process. Indexing involves creating a data structure that allows us to quickly retrieve the most similar sources to a given query. Hashing involves mapping the features of each source to a set of hash values. This allows us to quickly identify potential matches without having to compare the features of all sources. Another computational challenge is the cost of training the probabilistic model. This can be particularly challenging if the model is complex or if the dataset is large. To address this challenge, we can use techniques such as stochastic gradient descent or mini-batch training to reduce the computational cost of each iteration. We can also use techniques such as regularization to prevent overfitting and improve the generalization performance of the model. Also, consider dimensionality reduction techniques to address computational burdens. Methods like Principal Component Analysis (PCA) can reduce the number of features considered, making the computations more manageable.

Finally, it is crucial to consider the ethical implications of probabilistic attribution models. These models can be used to identify potential instances of plagiarism or copyright infringement, but they can also be used to make judgments about the originality and creativity of a work. It is important to use these models responsibly and to be aware of their limitations.

Remember, probabilistic models provide only a measure of likelihood, not definitive proof of attribution. They should be used as a tool to inform human judgment, not to replace it. Before deploying an attribution model, consider the potential biases that may be embedded in the data or the model itself. Biases can lead to unfair or discriminatory outcomes, particularly if the model is used to evaluate the work of individuals from underrepresented groups. Strive for transparency and explainability in your models. Users should understand how the model arrives at its conclusions and be able to challenge the results if they believe they are inaccurate or unfair.

3.2 Bayesian Attribution Bounds

Bayesian Attribution Bounds
Imagine you're a detective, but instead of solving crimes, you're untangling the threads of authorship, figuring out who contributed what to a creative work. That's essentially what we're doing with Bayesian attribution bounds, only instead of hunches and gut feelings, we're using the power of probability to make informed judgments. Bayesian attribution, at its core, offers a sophisticated framework for acknowledging the inherent uncertainties in determining authorship. It moves beyond simple yes/no answers to provide a spectrum of probabilities, reflecting the likelihood of different individuals or sources contributing to a piece of work. This approach acknowledges that attribution is rarely a black-and-white issue, especially in the complex digital landscape.

How does it work? We start by establishing a prior belief about who might be responsible for specific elements within a work. This prior could be based on historical data, expert opinions, or even simple assumptions. For example, in examining a jointly written scientific paper, the prior could reflect the known expertise of each author. One author might be a renowned statistician, leading to a higher prior probability of their contribution to the methodology section. Then, we analyze the evidence, the observable characteristics of the work itself, like writing style, code snippets, or artistic techniques. Each piece of evidence either strengthens or weakens our initial beliefs. This process of updating beliefs based on evidence is what distinguishes the Bayesian approach. The "Bayes' Theorem," the heart of this method, provides a mathematical formula for updating our prior beliefs in light of new evidence. This update results in a posterior probability, which represents our refined assessment of attribution. Essentially, Bayes' Theorem provides a systematic way to revise our initial hypotheses as we gather more information.

Consider a scenario involving musical composition. A new song is released, and it bears a striking resemblance to a previously published melody. A Bayesian framework allows us to quantify the likelihood that the new song infringes upon the original composition. The prior probability would incorporate factors such as the popularity of the original song (more popular songs are more likely to be copied) and the known tendencies of the composer of the new song (do they have a history of similar work?). The evidence might include a detailed analysis of the musical notes, rhythm, and harmonic structure of both songs. A close match would significantly increase the posterior probability of infringement, while substantial differences would lower it. The beauty of this method lies in its ability to incorporate diverse forms of evidence and expert opinions into a coherent probabilistic framework.

The real power of Bayesian attribution bounds lies in their ability to quantify uncertainty. Traditional attribution methods often provide a single, definitive answer, even when the evidence is ambiguous. Bayesian methods, on the other hand, provide a probability distribution, reflecting the range of possible attributions and their associated likelihoods. Imagine two coders working on a software project. A particular function is written, and it's not immediately clear who wrote which line. A Bayesian model could estimate the probability that each coder contributed to the function, perhaps with a range reflecting the uncertainty in the coding logs or individual styles. This probabilistic view provides a more nuanced and honest assessment of attribution, especially when clear-cut evidence is lacking.

The specification of priors is critical and can be a source of debate. A poorly chosen prior can bias the results, leading to inaccurate attributions. Therefore, sensitivity analyses are crucial. These involve testing the model with different priors to see how much the results change. If the posterior probabilities are highly sensitive to the choice of prior, it suggests that the evidence is not strong enough to overcome the initial assumptions. In such cases, caution is warranted in drawing firm conclusions. While it is important to choose priors that are both informative and defensible, it is equally crucial to acknowledge the subjectivity involved and to be transparent about the choices made.

Beyond simple attribution, Bayesian methods can also be used to establish bounds on attribution. A bound represents the maximum or minimum amount of credit that can be attributed to a particular individual or source. This is especially useful in legal contexts where precise attribution is required for copyright or patent purposes. Bayesian credible intervals can be used to define these bounds. A credible interval represents a range of values within which the true attribution likely falls, with a certain degree of confidence. For example, we might say that we are 95% confident that a particular author contributed between 60% and 80% of a given text. This range provides a more realistic and defensible assessment than a single point estimate.

Addressing data scarcity is a common challenge in attribution modeling. In many cases, we simply don't have enough information to definitively determine who contributed what. Bayesian methods provide a way to handle this uncertainty by incorporating prior beliefs and using regularization techniques to prevent overfitting the data. Regularization involves adding constraints to the model to prevent it from becoming too complex and sensitive to noise in the data. This helps to ensure that the model generalizes well to new data and provides more reliable attribution estimates. For instance, if analyzing the brushstrokes in a painting to determine the contributions of different artists, a prior belief about the typical number of brushstrokes in paintings by each artist could be incorporated to stabilize the estimation in the absence of extensive labeled data.

Computational demands can be another hurdle in applying Bayesian attribution bounds. Complex models with large datasets can require significant computational resources and time. However, advancements in computing power and optimization algorithms are making these methods increasingly feasible. Markov Chain Monte Carlo (MCMC) methods are commonly used to estimate posterior probabilities in Bayesian models. These methods involve simulating a large number of samples from the posterior distribution and using these samples to approximate the distribution. While MCMC methods can be computationally intensive, they are often the only way to estimate posterior probabilities in complex models.

Consider the case of collaborative software development where multiple programmers contribute code to a single project. Establishing clear attribution bounds is important for intellectual property protection and for accurately assessing individual contributions. A Bayesian model could be constructed to estimate the probability that each programmer contributed specific lines of code, based on factors such as their coding style, expertise, and the history of their contributions to the project. The model could then be used to establish credible intervals for each programmer's contribution, providing a range of plausible values that reflect the uncertainty in the data. This information could be used to inform licens-

ing agreements, compensation structures, and other decisions related to the project.
In conclusion, Bayesian attribution bounds offer a powerful and flexible framework for addressing the challenges of authorship in the digital age. By quantifying uncertainty, incorporating prior beliefs, and providing probabilistic estimates of attribution, these methods provide a more nuanced and defensible assessment than traditional approaches. While challenges remain in terms of data scarcity and computational demands, ongoing advancements in computing and statistical modeling are making Bayesian attribution bounds an increasingly valuable tool for protecting artistic works, resolving copyright disputes, and promoting responsible innovation. I hope this helps.

3.3 Statistical Significance Testing

The core of statistical significance testing in attribution lies in determining whether observed changes to a piece of work are likely due to intentional alteration or simply random variation. Let's consider an example: Imagine a musician creates a song, and later, someone else releases a similar track. To what extent does the new song infringe on the original artist's creative work? Statistical significance can offer some answers. It lets us test whether similarities between the two songs are so pronounced that they are unlikely to have arisen by chance. This involves formulating a null hypothesis—for instance, "there is no relationship between the two songs beyond what would be expected by random chance." We then analyze the musical elements (melody, harmony, rhythm, etc.) to calculate a test statistic, such as a t-statistic or a chi-squared statistic, which quantifies the differences or similarities. If the resulting p-value (the probability of observing the data if the null hypothesis is true) is below a pre-determined significance level (alpha, typically 0.05), we reject the null hypothesis and conclude that there is statistically significant evidence to suggest that the observed similarities are not merely random.

Delving deeper, the choice of statistical test depends heavily on the nature of the data and the specific attribution question being asked. If we are comparing the frequency of certain phrases or themes in two pieces of writing, a chi-squared test might be appropriate to determine if the observed frequencies differ significantly from what would be expected if the two works were independent. If we are comparing the average length of sentences or the distribution of word usage, a t-test or analysis of variance (ANOVA) might be more suitable. In these cases, you might use specialized software and manually count or extract the attributes to compare. If the test result produces a statistically significant outcome, you can say something like, "The observed similarities in phrase usage are statistically significant at p < 0.01, providing strong evidence against the assumption that these texts are independent creations." This kind of language directly supports an argument about the dependence of one piece of work on another, a key element in attribution disputes.

However, it's crucial to remember that statistical significance does not automatically equate to legal or ethical attribution. A statistically significant similarity might still be attributable to common influences or genre conventions. For example, two romantic comedies might share similar plot structures or character archetypes, which, while statistically frequent, don't necessarily imply infringement. Furthermore, a low p-value doesn't tell us the magnitude or importance of the observed difference. A very large dataset might yield statistically significant results even for trivial differences. Therefore, it's vital to consider the effect size—a measure of the practical importance of the observed effect—alongside statistical significance. A common effect size measure is Cohen's d, which quantifies the difference between two means in terms of standard deviations. A Cohen's d of 0.8, for example, would indicate a large effect size. In the context of attribution, an effect size might measure the proportion of unique phrases copied or the degree of structural similarity.

Considering data limitations is also critical. Small sample sizes can lead to low statistical power, meaning we might fail to detect real differences even when they exist. Conversely, very large datasets can artificially inflate statistical significance, making even minor similarities appear meaningful. It is essential to perform a power analysis to determine the appropriate sample size needed to detect a meaningful effect with a reasonable level of confidence. One can use simulation techniques to estimate power by generating artificial datasets under different assumptions about the effect size and sample size. To address these issues, consider resampling methods like bootstrapping, where you repeatedly sample from your dataset with replacement to estimate the variability of your test statistic. Bootstrapping is particularly useful when the assumptions of traditional statistical tests are not met or when sample sizes are small.

Let's think about Bayesian methods to attribution bounds. In Bayesian statistical testing, we start with a prior belief about the probability of a hypothesis being true and then update this belief based on the observed data to arrive at a posterior probability. In the context of authorship attribution, this might involve starting with a prior belief about the likelihood that two texts were written by the same author and then updating this belief based on the observed stylistic similarities. Bayesian hypothesis testing offers several advantages over traditional frequentist methods. It allows us to directly calculate the probability of a hypothesis being true, rather than just rejecting or failing to reject a null hypothesis. It also provides a natural way to incorporate prior knowledge into the analysis. However, Bayesian methods also have their challenges, including the need to specify a prior distribution and the computational complexity of calculating posterior probabilities. A common approach to Bayesian hypothesis testing is to use Bayes factors, which quantify the relative evidence for one hypothesis over another. A Bayes factor greater than 1 indicates evidence in favor of the first hypothesis, while a Bayes factor less than 1 indicates evidence in favor of the second hypothesis.

Applying these principles, imagine a scenario where two software developers have created similar code libraries. One claims the other copied their code. To statistically assess the attribution, we might start by defining a null hypothesis: the similarities between the two code libraries are purely coincidental. We could then analyze the frequency of particular code structures, variable names, or algorithm implementations. Using statistical tests, like the chi-squared test, we can determine the likelihood of observing such similarities if the null hypothesis were true. If the p-value is low (e.g., below 0.05), we might reject the null hypothesis, suggesting the code libraries are not independent. But, statistical tests alone cannot tell the whole story. We need to incorporate expert judgment, evaluate the effect size, and consider alternative explanations, such as the use of shared open-source libraries.

A critical aspect of statistical significance testing in attribution is addressing potential biases. For example, confirmation bias might lead us to selectively focus on similarities that support our pre-existing beliefs. To mitigate this, it's crucial to use objective and transparent methods for data collection and analysis, and to clearly document all assumptions and decisions made during the process. Also, consider the possibility of confounding variables – factors that influence both the original work and the potential infringement. Perhaps both authors drew inspiration from the same source material. Accounting for these confounders requires careful consideration of the broader context and may involve using more sophisticated statistical techniques, such as regression analysis or propensity score matching. These methods allow us to control for the effects of confounding variables and isolate the relationship between the original work and the potential infringement. Ultimately, statistical significance testing provides a valuable tool for assessing attribution, but it must be used judiciously, in conjunction with other evidence, and with careful consideration of its limitations. It provides a rigorous framework for evaluating claims of authorship and infringement.

3.4 Addressing Data Scarcity

Data scarcity looms large when we try to create statistical attribution bounds for creative works. Consider this: a completely new art form emerges, blending virtual reality with ancient storytelling techniques. There's no existing data on how such works are typically attributed, how much modification is acceptable, or even what constitutes a derivative work in this novel space. Traditional statistical methods, which rely on vast datasets to identify patterns and establish probabilities, falter. We can't simply apply standard plagiarism detection algorithms, because the very nature of the work defies prior categorization. Instead, a thoughtful, multi-pronged strategy must be employed to navigate this data-poor environment.

The first step is to leverage all available, albeit indirect, data. This means broadening our search beyond the specific domain of the creative work. For our VR storytelling example, we might look at data from related fields: the film industry (to understand adaptation rights), the gaming industry (to understand modification in interactive narratives), and traditional publishing (to understand plagiarism conventions). Each of these areas possesses some applicable principles, but none directly mirror our novel situation. Therefore, we must carefully extract relevant information and adapt it to the new context. This requires a deep understanding of the underlying principles of attribution, not just the surface-level rules.

Active learning becomes crucial in scenarios with limited data. Instead of passively waiting for data to accumulate, we need to actively generate it. This can be accomplished through carefully designed experiments and surveys. For example, we could present a panel of experts (artists, lawyers, and consumers) with different variations of the VR story and ask them to assess the degree to which the original author's contribution is still evident. These subjective assessments, while not perfect, provide valuable data points for building a statistical model. The key is to design these experiments in a way that maximizes the information gained from each data point. This might involve using techniques like adaptive sampling, where we focus our efforts on areas where our model is most uncertain. We could also create "synthetic data" through simulations, artificially generating variations of the work and attributing authorship based on pre-defined rules. While this synthetic data isn't real, it can help to train our model and identify potential biases.

Another strategy is to incorporate prior knowledge and expert opinions into the statistical model. Bayesian methods are particularly well-suited for this purpose. They allow us to start with a prior belief about the attribution process and then update that belief as we gather more data. This is especially useful when data is scarce, as it allows us to leverage existing knowledge to guide our analysis. For example, we might start with a prior belief that any modification exceeding a certain percentage constitutes a derivative work. As we collect data, we can refine this belief based on the observed patterns. However, it's crucial to acknowledge and address potential biases within the prior knowledge. Expert opinions, while valuable, can be influenced by personal preferences or industry conventions. Therefore, we must carefully evaluate the source of our prior knowledge and ensure that it is as objective as possible. Moreover, embrace the power of qualitative analysis. In the absence of extensive quantitative data, qualitative insights can be invaluable. Conduct in-depth interviews with creators, legal experts, and consumers to understand their perceptions of attribution in the specific context. Analyze case studies of similar situations, even if they are not directly analogous. Look for recurring themes and patterns that can inform your understanding of the attribution process. This qualitative analysis can help to identify key factors that influence attribution decisions, such as the originality of the work, the degree of modification, and the commercial value of the derivative work. This information can then be incorporated into the statistical model as variables or constraints.

Consider also adopting transfer learning techniques. Transfer learning involves leveraging knowledge gained from one domain to improve performance in another, related domain. In our data-scarce VR storytelling example, we might use a model trained on a large dataset of film adaptations to bootstrap our understanding of attribution in VR. The film adaptation model can provide a starting point for identifying relevant features and relationships, which can then be refined using the limited data available for VR storytelling. This can significantly reduce the amount of data needed to train a robust attribution model. However, it's crucial to carefully evaluate the applicability of the transfer learning approach. The source domain should be sufficiently similar to the target domain to ensure that the transferred knowledge is relevant and accurate.

Furthermore, address the ethical considerations of data scarcity. When data is limited, there is a greater risk of bias and unfairness. Statistical models trained on small datasets may not accurately reflect the diversity of creative works and authorship styles. This can lead to discriminatory outcomes, where certain authors or types of works are unfairly penalized. Therefore, it's essential to be transparent about the limitations of the statistical model and to take steps to mitigate potential biases. This might involve using fairness-aware machine learning techniques, which are designed to minimize disparities between different groups. It might also involve incorporating human oversight into the attribution process, to ensure that the statistical model is not making decisions in isolation.

Finally, remember that attribution is not always a zero-sum game. In many cases, it's possible to give credit to both the original author and the creator of the derivative work. This is particularly important in collaborative projects, where multiple authors contribute to the final product. Statistical attribution bounds can be used to determine the relative contributions of each author, ensuring that everyone receives appropriate recognition. The goal is not to simply identify who is the "true" author, but rather to understand the complex web of influences and contributions that shape creative works. By embracing a more nuanced approach to attribution, we can foster creativity and innovation while protecting the rights of authors. The process is evolutionary, not revolutionary, and each adaptation further refines our understanding of authorship in the digital age. We must adopt these strategies and carefully adapt them to each unique situation where data is sparse.

3.5 Computational Challenges

Computational challenges are at the heart of implementing robust statistical attribution bounds. While the theoretical frameworks offer a powerful approach to safeguarding authorship, their practical application often runs into significant hurdles, primarily due to the computational resources required. These challenges span from the sheer volume of data that needs to be analyzed to the complexity of the algorithms used for probabilistic modeling and statistical testing. The initial obstacle lies in data acquisition and preprocessing. To accurately determine attribution bounds, we need a vast amount of relevant data. This may include the original work, potentially infringing works, authorial style markers, usage statistics, and contextual information. Gathering this data can be a monumental task, especially when dealing with works that are distributed across various platforms or exist in different formats. Once collected, the data needs to be cleaned, normalized, and transformed into a format suitable for analysis. This often involves complex natural language processing techniques, feature extraction methods, and data integration strategies. For example, consider a scenario where we want to determine the attribution bound for a piece of music. We would need to gather audio samples of the original song, potential infringing pieces, and a database of musical features. Preprocessing this data would involve audio segmentation, feature extraction (e.g., melody, harmony, rhythm), and normalization to account for differences in recording quality and instrumentation. Each of these steps carries its own computational cost, requiring specialized software and hardware.

Further complicating matters is the choice of statistical model. Probabilistic attribution models, such as Bayesian networks and Markov models, are often used to quantify the likelihood of authorship given certain features. However, these models can be computationally expensive to train and evaluate, especially when dealing with high-dimensional data. The complexity of the model grows exponentially with the number of features and the size of the dataset. Bayesian methods, in particular, require sampling from posterior distributions, which can be computationally intensive. Approximations such as Markov Chain Monte Carlo (MCMC) methods are often used, but these can still be slow to converge and require careful tuning to ensure accuracy. Imagine trying to apply a Bayesian network to determine the authorship of a piece of text. The model would need to learn the relationships between words, phrases, and authorial style markers. With thousands of potential features and a large corpus of text, the computational cost of training such a model can be prohibitive.

The need for statistical significance testing adds another layer of complexity. To establish attribution bounds with a certain level of confidence, we need to perform hypothesis tests to determine whether the observed differences between works are statistically significant. This involves calculating p-values and confidence intervals, which can be computationally intensive, especially when dealing with complex statistical models. Bootstrapping and permutation tests are often used to estimate the distribution of test statistics, but these methods require resampling the data many times, further increasing the computational burden. For example, when comparing two pieces of code to detect plagiarism, we might use statistical significance testing to determine whether the similarity between the code structures is likely to have occurred by chance. This would involve comparing the observed similarity score to a distribution of similarity scores generated from randomly permuted code sequences.

Data scarcity presents a unique set of computational challenges. In many cases, we may not have enough data to train a robust statistical model. This is particularly true when dealing with novel authorship scenarios or when the original work is not widely available. In such cases, we need to employ techniques such as transfer learning, data augmentation, or semi-supervised learning to overcome the data limitations.

Transfer learning involves leveraging knowledge gained from related tasks to improve the performance of our model. Data augmentation involves generating synthetic data to increase the size of our training set. Semi-supervised learning involves using unlabeled data to improve the accuracy of our model. These techniques can be computationally expensive, but they are often necessary to achieve acceptable performance when data is scarce.

The interpretation of statistical results in a legally defensible manner also raises significant challenges. Even with sophisticated statistical models, there is always a degree of uncertainty in the attribution bounds. Communicating this uncertainty in a way that is understandable and persuasive to a legal audience is crucial. Visualizations, such as confidence intervals and probability distributions, can be helpful in this regard. However, it is important to avoid overstating the certainty of the results or drawing unwarranted conclusions. Furthermore, it is essential to consider the potential for bias in the data and the model. Statistical models are only as good as the data they are trained on, and if the data is biased, the results will be biased as well. Careful attention must be paid to ensuring that the data is representative of the population of interest and that the model is not unfairly penalizing or favoring certain authors.

To address these computational challenges, several strategies can be employed. First, it is important to leverage efficient algorithms and data structures. Many statistical algorithms have been optimized for performance, and using these optimized implementations can significantly reduce the computational cost. For example, using sparse matrix representations can greatly improve the performance of linear algebra operations on high-dimensional data. Second, it is important to parallelize the computation. Many statistical tasks can be divided into smaller subtasks that can be executed concurrently on multiple processors or machines. This can significantly reduce the overall runtime, especially for large datasets. Third, it is important to use cloud computing resources. Cloud platforms offer a wide range of computational resources, including virtual machines, GPUs, and specialized hardware accelerators. Leveraging these resources can allow us to tackle computationally intensive tasks that would be impossible to perform on a single machine. Finally, it is important to develop new statistical methods that are specifically designed to address the challenges of attribution analysis. This includes developing more efficient algorithms, more robust statistical models, and more interpretable visualization techniques. The ongoing research in this area is essential for advancing the state of the art in attribution analysis and ensuring that authors' rights are protected in the digital age.

In conclusion, establishing statistical attribution bounds presents significant computational challenges, ranging from data acquisition and preprocessing to model training and evaluation. Addressing these challenges requires a combination of efficient algorithms, parallel computing, cloud resources, and innovative statistical methods. Only by overcoming these hurdles can we hope to develop robust and reliable attribution frameworks that can effectively safeguard authors' production in the digital age.

4 Chapter 4: Causal Inference and Attribution

Attribution, in its simplest form, answers the question of "who created this?". However, in today's complex digital ecosystem, that question often demands more than a simple name. We need to understand how a creation came to be, and what elements are fundamentally derived from an original source. This requires delving into the realm of causality. We are no longer simply looking at correlations; we're seeking to establish direct links between actions (interventions) and their effect on authorship. How much does a modification change the attribution? Does incorporating elements of one work into another dilute or enhance the original author's claim? These are the questions causal inference allows us to address with far greater precision.

Causal models provide a structured framework to represent these complex relationships. Think of a directed graph, where nodes represent variables related to authorship – the original work, modifications, derivative works, even the actions of different actors. Arrows indicate causal influences. For instance, an arrow might point from "Original Song" to "Remix," indicating that the original song directly influences the creation of the remix. However, to be truly useful, these models must go beyond just representation; they must allow us to answer specific causal questions. This often involves employing techniques like structural equation modeling or potential outcomes frameworks to estimate the magnitude of causal effects. A core aspect is identifying potential confounding variables. A confounding variable is something that influences both the 'cause' and the 'effect', leading to spurious correlations. For example, if two songs become popular because they are both used in a very famous TikTok video, it might seem like one influenced the other, when in reality it was the video influencing them both. Ignoring confounders can lead to incorrect conclusions about attribution. Once a solid model is established, we can begin to explore the impact of interventions on attribution.

An intervention, in the context of authorship, is any action that alters the original work or its context. This could range from simple edits to complete transformations. A crucial element of causal inference is understanding how these interventions affect the attribution owed to the original author. For example, consider a photograph that is heavily edited and colorized. Does the colorization diminish the original photographer's claim? What if the colorization is so transformative that it creates a completely new aesthetic? Interventions are not simply about the presence of change, but the nature and magnitude of that change. One approach is to apply so-called 'do-calculus' on our causal model. This allows us to simulate the effect of an intervention by mathematically manipulating the model to reflect the enforced change. We can then compare the predicted outcome under intervention to the predicted outcome without intervention, giving us a measure of the intervention's causal effect. This helps determine how much the intervention altered the work and, therefore, to what degree it changed the attribution.

However, interventions rarely happen in isolation. It's more common to see a chain of interventions or multiple parties contributing to a final product. This introduces the need for a sophisticated analysis of mediation. Mediation analysis helps us understand the pathway through which an intervention affects attribution. For instance, imagine an AI algorithm is trained on an author's work, and then used to generate a new text. The author's work is the initial 'cause', the AI algorithm is the mediator, and the generated text is the 'effect'. Mediation analysis allows us to determine how much of the effect (the generated text) is due to the author's work, through the AI algorithm. This is critical for establishing fair attribution when multiple agents are involved in the creative process.

Counterfactual reasoning takes us into the realm of "what if" scenarios. This is the ability to imagine alternative realities and explore how attribution would change under different circumstances. The central question here is: What would have happened to the derivative work if a particular intervention had not occurred? For example, suppose a song samples a melody from an earlier work. Counterfactual reasoning compels us to ask: How similar would the new song be if the sample had not been included? Would it have achieved the same level of success? Counterfactuals are inherently hypothetical, making them challenging to assess. However, sophisticated statistical techniques, combined with careful modeling, allow us to approximate these scenarios.

One commonly used approach involves the construction of potential outcomes. For each individual work, we envision two potential outcomes: one where the intervention occurs (the actual outcome), and one where it does not (the counterfactual outcome). The difference between these two outcomes represents the causal effect of the intervention for that specific work. This approach is particularly useful when dealing with unique works of art, where replication or experimentation is impossible. The goal of counterfactual reasoning isn't to provide definitive answers, but rather to offer a range of plausible scenarios and estimate the likelihood of each. This allows for a more nuanced and informed discussion about attribution in complex cases. It is important to acknowledge that counterfactual reasoning always contains inherent uncertainty. We are, after all, speculating about what might have been. Thus, it's essential to frame counterfactual arguments in terms of probabilities and to acknowledge the limitations of our knowledge. Even so, this kind of approach can greatly help when dealing with complicated cases.

In essence, causal inference provides a powerful toolset for navigating the complex world of attribution. By going beyond mere correlations and focusing on causal relationships, we can achieve a more accurate and equitable assessment of authorship in the digital age. This is particularly important as technology continues to blur the lines between creation and modification, making it all the more essential to understand how interventions impact attribution. By applying these methods rigorously, we can develop frameworks for safeguarding authors' production and ensuring that credit is given where credit is truly due. This chapter provides a first step in understanding the complex and nuanced approach for handling sensitive cases.

4.1 Causal Models for Authorship

Causal inference offers a powerful lens through which we can understand authorship attribution, moving beyond mere correlation to establish cause-and-effect relationships. This chapter delves into how causal models can be applied to determine the true impact of various interventions on a piece of work, thereby informing our judgment about who deserves credit for what aspects of its creation. This is especially pertinent in complex scenarios involving multiple contributors, derivative works, and even the influence of pre-existing sources. Without a solid grasp of causal relationships, we risk attributing contributions incorrectly, potentially leading to unfair or inaccurate assessments of authorship.

Causal models allow us to explicitly represent the relationships between different variables involved in the creation and modification of a work. These variables might include the contributions of different individuals, the influence of external factors, or even the application of specific techniques or processes. By mapping out these relationships, we can then use statistical methods to estimate the causal effects of each variable on the final outcome. For example, we might want to determine the effect of a particular author's edits on the overall quality or originality of a text. Or, we could explore how the use of a specific dataset impacted the style or content of a generated image. This type of analysis allows us to differentiate between mere correlation and genuine causation, providing a more accurate picture of who contributed what and to what extent. It is not enough to simply observe that a certain author's involvement coincides with a certain outcome. We need to establish whether their involvement actually caused that outcome.

An essential aspect of applying causal models to authorship is understanding the concept of intervention. In this context, an intervention refers to a deliberate act that alters one or more variables in the causal model. For example, imagine a piece of music that is co-written by two musicians. One musician lays down the main melody (Musician A) and the other adds harmonies and complex arrangements (Musician B). If we were to remove Musician B's contributions, this would constitute an intervention. By observing the state of the music without Musician B's harmonies and arrangements, we can isolate the causal effect of Musician B's contribution. Did those harmonies make the song more commercially viable? More technically sophisticated? This is important when determining attribution, because by looking at what each person does we can measure the significance of their collaboration. Interventions in causal models allow us to simulate these scenarios and estimate the impact of different individuals' work. This is a far more rigorous approach than simply comparing the final product to the work of each individual in isolation.

Counterfactual reasoning is another powerful tool within the framework of causal inference. Counterfactuals involve considering what would have happened if a certain event had not occurred. In the context of authorship, this could mean asking questions like "What would this novel have been like if this particular editor had not made their suggested changes?" or "What would the painting have looked like if this artist had not used that specific brushstroke?". These are not merely hypothetical questions; they can be addressed using causal models. By simulating different scenarios and comparing the predicted outcomes, we can gain a better understanding of the impact of specific contributions. This is especially valuable when assessing the originality of a derivative work. We can use counterfactual reasoning to assess whether the changes made by the new author were truly transformative or whether they simply built upon the foundation laid by the original author.

Consider a scenario where a student submits an essay that contains passages similar to existing online articles. A simple plagiarism checker might flag the essay as containing plagiarized content. However, a causal approach would delve deeper. It would explore whether the student directly copied and pasted the content (a causal link) or whether they independently arrived at similar ideas through their own research and reasoning (a correlation, but not necessarily a causal link). Further, it would assess whether the student's contributions were sufficiently original to warrant authorship, even if some elements were similar to pre-existing works. Perhaps the student used the existing articles as a starting point and then developed their own unique analysis and arguments.

One significant challenge in applying causal models to authorship is accurately defining and measuring the relevant variables. It can be difficult to quantify subjective aspects of creative work, such as originality, style, and artistic merit. However, advances in natural language processing and machine learning offer promising avenues for automating some of these tasks. For example, sentiment analysis tools can be used to assess the emotional tone of a text, while stylistic analysis tools can be used to identify the author's characteristic writing style. Additionally, data on audience reception and critical reviews can be used as proxies for measuring the overall impact and value of a work. To be used, these measurement tools must be validated against human judgments, to confirm that they are capturing meaningful aspects of authorship.

Another challenge is dealing with confounding variables, which are factors that influence both the alleged cause and effect. In authorship attribution, confounding variables can arise from shared influences, common sources of information, or even the inherent limitations of a particular medium. For example, two artists working in the same style may produce similar works, not because they directly copied each other, but because they were both influenced by the same artistic movement. Similarly, two authors writing about the same topic may use similar language and concepts simply because they are drawing on the same body of knowledge. To mitigate the effects of confounding variables, researchers can use a variety of statistical techniques, such as regression analysis and propensity score matching. The aim is to isolate the true causal effect of the variable of interest, while controlling for the influence of other factors.

The application of causal models to authorship has significant implications for intellectual property law and copyright. By providing a more rigorous and accurate framework for assessing authorship, we can create fairer and more effective laws that protect the rights of creators while also promoting innovation and creativity. Consider the issue of fair use. Current copyright law allows for the use of copyrighted material for purposes such as criticism, commentary, and parody. However, the boundaries of fair use are often unclear, and courts must weigh a variety of factors to determine whether a particular use is permissible. Causal models can help to clarify these boundaries by providing a more objective assessment of the transformative nature of the use.

To conclude, causal inference offers a powerful approach to understand authorship, moving beyond correlation to establish cause-and-effect relationships. By embracing the principles of causal models, we can move towards a more nuanced and accurate understanding of who deserves credit for what, especially as the lines of authorship continue to blur in the digital age. As we continue to develop and refine these techniques, we can look forward to a future where authorship is more fairly and equitably recognized and rewarded.

4.2 Intervention and Attribution

Understanding authorship through the lens of causal inference requires a shift from merely observing correlations to actively probing the underlying mechanisms of influence. It's not enough to simply note that two works share similar elements; we must delve into why those similarities exist, and whether one directly caused the other. This chapter illuminates how interventions – deliberate actions taken on a source work – affect the degree of attribution owed to the original author and explores the vital role of counterfactual reasoning in navigating complex authorship disputes.

Causal models provide a structured way to represent the relationships between different components of authorship. Think of it like this: a causal model for a song might include variables like "original melody," "harmonic progression," "lyrical themes," and "artist's interpretation." We can then use arrows to depict the influence of one variable on another. For example, the "original melody" might directly influence the "harmonic progression," and both might contribute to the overall "artist's interpretation." These models are more than just diagrams; they are mathematical representations that allow us to quantify the strength of these causal connections. Once we've built a causal model, we can start to explore the effects of interventions.

Now, an intervention, in our context, is a deliberate act that alters one or more aspects of a work. Examples range from sampling a beat from an existing song to translating a novel into another language, or even using parts of the work in another piece of work. The key is that the intervention is intentional. When we intervene on a work, we're essentially changing one of the variables in our causal model. What makes intervention crucial to attribution is its ability to isolate the specific impact of an action on the derivative work. It allows us to say, with a degree of confidence, that "this much of the new work is directly attributable to the original because of this specific intervention." This level of specificity is essential for fair and accurate attribution. The more significant and transformative the intervention, the less attribution may be due to the original author, but the causality must be proven.

Consider a scenario where an artist samples a short musical phrase from an obscure jazz record in their new hit song. A simple correlation analysis might identify the presence of that phrase, but it wouldn't tell us much about its impact on the song's success. By using causal inference, we could model the influence of the sampled phrase on the overall song structure, its memorability, and its appeal to listeners. We could even run experiments, for example, by creating versions of the song with and without the sample to see how it affects listener ratings. Such rigorous analysis would provide stronger evidence of the sample's contribution, thereby informing the appropriate level of attribution.

This leads us to counterfactual reasoning, a powerful tool for understanding "what if" scenarios. In the context of attribution, counterfactuals allow us to ask questions like: "What would the derivative work have been like if the intervention had never occurred?" By exploring these hypothetical scenarios, we can gain a deeper understanding of the causal role played by the original work. Imagine that a writer incorporates a passage from a historical document into their novel. If we want to assess the extent to which the original author deserves attribution, we might ask: "How essential was that passage to the novel's narrative? Could the writer have achieved the same effect using different sources or their own words?" If the passage was merely decorative or easily replaceable, then the original author might deserve less attribution than if it was integral to the plot or theme.

To effectively apply counterfactual reasoning, we often rely on techniques like "do-calculus," a mathematical framework for manipulating causal models. Do-calculus allows us to simulate the effects of interventions and explore counterfactual scenarios in a rigorous and systematic way. While the mathematics can be complex, the underlying idea is straightforward: we want to isolate the causal effect of a particular intervention by comparing the actual outcome to what would have happened in its absence. This comparison helps us determine the "but-for" cause – the event that, if it had not occurred, the outcome would have been different.

However, implementing causal inference in attribution is not without its challenges. One major obstacle is the difficulty of constructing accurate causal models. Unlike controlled experiments in a laboratory, we often cannot directly manipulate authorship in the real world. We have to rely on observational data, which can be noisy and incomplete. Furthermore, causal relationships can be complex and intertwined, making it difficult to disentangle the effects of different factors. For instance, a song's success may depend not only on the original melody but also on the artist's performance, the production quality, and the marketing campaign.

Another challenge is the subjectivity involved in defining and measuring "similarity" between works. Even with a sophisticated causal model, we still need to determine what constitutes a meaningful intervention and how to quantify its impact. This often requires human judgment, which can be influenced by biases and personal preferences. Consider the case of musical plagiarism, where experts often disagree on whether two songs are "substantially similar." This highlights the need for clear and objective criteria for assessing similarity, which can be difficult to achieve in practice.

Despite these challenges, causal inference offers a powerful framework for understanding and resolving attribution disputes. By moving beyond simple correlations and embracing a more nuanced understanding of causality, we can create a more fair and equitable system for recognizing and rewarding creative contributions. It encourages a deeper examination of the creative process, forcing us to confront the difficult questions of influence, originality, and the value of individual contributions. This rigorous, evidence-based approach can help prevent unfair claims of plagiarism, protect the rights of original authors, and foster a more collaborative and innovative creative environment. It encourages creators to build upon existing works in a responsible way, acknowledging their sources while contributing something new and unique. It's a shift toward understanding authorship not as a static entity but as a dynamic process of influence and transformation.

4.3 Counterfactual Reasoning

Counterfactual reasoning offers a powerful lens through which to examine authorship attribution, particularly in cases where the lineage of a work is contested or complex. Instead of merely observing what did happen – the modifications, additions, or transformations a source work underwent – counterfactual analysis asks what would have happened had a particular action or intervention not occurred. This "what if" perspective allows us to delve deeper into the causal relationships between an original creation and its derivative works, thereby providing a more nuanced understanding of who deserves credit for which elements. To understand how it works, we must first know how to establish causal relationships. This can be achieved by analyzing the changes in the derivative work, trying to link each specific change to a possible cause, for example, the presence of a paragraph in the original text. This requires an understanding of the topic and the specific areas involved to be sure to link it with the right reasons.
Central to counterfactual reasoning in attribution is the con-

cept of intervention. An intervention is a specific action or event that alters the course of a work's development. For instance, adding a new chapter to a book, remixing a song, or modifying a piece of software's code are all examples of interventions. When evaluating attribution, we are often interested in determining the causal effect of these interventions. Did the addition of that new chapter significantly alter the overall meaning and value of the book, such that the person who added it deserves a substantial portion of the credit? Or was it merely a minor addition that had little impact on the original author's contribution? It can be easy to find yourself lost in an ocean of confusion without any expertise, but it is important to stay focused on what you are searching for, by asking the right questions. You can question the impact that a specific part had, if it's something that enhances or just modifies.

To answer these questions using counterfactual reasoning, we construct a counterfactual scenario. This is a hypothetical situation where the intervention in question did not occur. We then compare the actual outcome (the derivative work as it exists) to the counterfactual outcome (what the derivative work would have been like without the intervention). The difference between these two outcomes represents the causal effect of the intervention. Let's say a musician samples a five-second riff from an existing song and builds an entire new track around it. The actual outcome is the new track, with the sampled riff embedded within it. The counterfactual outcome is what the new track would have sounded like if the musician had not used the sample. Would it have been just as successful?

Would it have had the same artistic impact? If the riff is integral to the new song's appeal, then the original composer arguably deserves a significant portion of the attribution. If, on the other hand, the new song is successful largely due to the musician's own creative contributions, then the original composer's attribution might be more limited.

However, applying counterfactual reasoning to attribution is not without its challenges. One major hurdle is the inherent difficulty of constructing accurate counterfactual scenarios. It's often impossible to know precisely what a derivative work would have been like had a particular intervention not occurred. There are numerous alternative paths the creator could have taken, each leading to a different outcome. To address this, we often rely on expert judgment, historical analysis, and, increasingly, data-driven methods. Experts in a particular field (musicologists, literary scholars, software engineers, etc.) can provide informed opinions on the likely impact of different interventions. Analyzing similar cases from the past can offer valuable insights into how comparable modifications have affected attribution. Data-driven approaches, such as machine learning models trained on large datasets of creative works, can potentially predict the counterfactual outcome based on the characteristics of the original work and the nature of the intervention. To be able to assess this specific impact, we should consider different parameters, such as: the change in the content's quality after an intervention, and the change in the reach of the modified content compared to the original one.

Another key consideration is the level of abstraction at which we define the intervention. An intervention can be defined very narrowly (e.g., changing a single word in a sentence) or very broadly (e.g., rewriting an entire chapter). The choice of abstraction level can significantly affect the outcome of the counterfactual analysis. A minor change might have a negligible impact on the overall attribution, while a more substantial revision could warrant a greater share of the credit. The ideal level of abstraction depends on the specific context and the goals of the attribution analysis. In some cases, a granular analysis of individual changes may be necessary to determine the precise contribution of each author. In other cases, a broader assessment of the overall impact of an intervention may be sufficient. The type of work and the changes needed for it will be an important factor, such as the difficulty, the time required, and the expertise.

Moreover, counterfactual reasoning must be sensitive to the temporal order of events. The impact of an intervention can depend on when it occurred in the creation process. An early intervention that shapes the overall direction of a work may have a greater causal effect than a later intervention that merely refines existing elements. For example, a screenwriter who comes up with the initial concept and outline for a film may deserve more credit than a screenwriter who is brought in later to polish the dialogue, even if both contribute significantly to the final product. To account for this, counterfactual analyses should consider the chronological sequence of interventions and their cumulative impact on the work's development. For example, a change in the first steps will have a greater impact compared to changing it later.

Finally, it's important to recognize that counterfactual reasoning is not a purely objective exercise. It involves subjective judgments and interpretations, particularly when assessing the artistic or intellectual value of different contributions. Different people may have different opinions on what a derivative work would have been like without a particular intervention, and on the relative importance of different contributions. Therefore, it is crucial to be transparent about the assumptions and biases that underlie the counterfactual analysis, and to consider multiple perspectives when evaluating attribution.

In conclusion, counterfactual reasoning provides a valuable framework for analyzing authorship attribution by focusing on the causal relationships between original works and their derivative creations. By considering what would have happened had certain interventions not occurred, we can gain a more nuanced understanding of the contributions of different authors and make more informed judgments about who deserves credit for which elements. While challenges remain in constructing accurate counterfactual scenarios and accounting for subjective interpretations, the principles of causal inference offer a powerful tool for navigating the complexities of attribution in the digital age. We should always remember that, as with anything, counterfactual reasoning is not the definitive solution and should be considered as another element to consider.

5 Chapter 5: Information Theoretic Bounds

Information theory provides a powerful lens through which we can examine the problem of attribution, shifting the focus from simply detecting similarities to quantifying the amount of information retained from the original work in a derivative. This shift is critical because attribution isn't simply a binary question of whether copying occurred; it's a matter of how much of the original author's contribution remains present, and whether that remaining contribution warrants continued attribution. As such, using information theoretic concepts allows us to create bounds that are inherently quantitative and thus potentially more objective than subjective interpretations of similarity.

Entropy, in the context of attribution, becomes a measure of authorship uncertainty. High entropy means there's significant doubt about who contributed what to a particular work, which could arise from extensive modification, complex collaboration, or the obfuscating effects of certain processes. Imagine a painter who heavily reworks an underpainting created by another artist. The final painting may bear little resemblance to the original underpainting, resulting in high entropy regarding the underpainter's contribution. Conversely, low entropy suggests a high degree of certainty regarding the attribution of specific elements. For example, a direct quote from a famous author, clearly attributed, would have low entropy regarding its source. Mathematically, entropy, often denoted as H(X) for a random variable X representing authorship, is calculated based on the probabilities of different authorship assignments. If one author is overwhelmingly likely to be responsible for a work, entropy will be low. If many authors could plausibly be credited, entropy will be high. The goal, then, is to establish bounds on acceptable levels of entropy in derivative works; an entropy level that exceeds a predetermined threshold might suggest a violation of attribution principles. We should determine the point at which the uncertainty surrounding the original author's contribution becomes unacceptably high. This threshold would need to consider the nature of the original work, the context of its use, and prevailing legal standards.

Mutual information offers a more direct measure of the relationship between the original work and the derivative. While entropy quantifies uncertainty within a single source, mutual information quantifies the reduction in uncertainty about one source given knowledge of another. In simpler terms, it measures how much knowing about the derivative work tells us about the original work, and vice-versa. If the derivative work contains a substantial amount of information directly traceable to the original, the mutual information will be high. If the derivative work is highly original and independent, the mutual information will be low. A remix of a song that heavily samples the original would have high mutual information. A novel inspired by a historical event would likely have low mutual information, even if inspired by it, because most of the information is new and independent of the original event account. The key is to define what level of mutual information represents an unacceptable degree of dependence on the original work, requiring attribution. Again, this threshold isn't absolute; it depends on the context of the work and the purpose of the derivative.

Channel capacity, a concept borrowed from communication theory, can be analogized to the maximum amount of "authorship information" that can be transmitted from the original work to the derivative work without violating attribution bounds. Think of the original work as the sender, the derivative work as the receiver, and the process of creation/modification as the channel. Noise in the channel represents modifications, alterations, or creative additions that obscure the original author's contribution. The channel capacity represents the theoretical limit on how much of the original author's "signal" can pass through the "noise" and still be recognizably attributed. If the derivative work attempts to transmit more authorship information than the channel capacity allows (given a certain noise level), it could be considered an infringement on the original author's rights. For example, if a student copies a paragraph nearly verbatim from a paper without attribution, they are trying to transmit nearly 100%

of the original author's information, which is far beyond the "channel capacity" allowed in academic settings. The channel capacity is influenced by the noise level and characteristics of the channel itself. In creative contexts, the "noise" could be significant alterations, artistic interpretations, or transformative additions. A parody, for instance, might introduce substantial "noise" in the channel, reducing the effective channel capacity and allowing for more extensive borrowing without necessarily requiring direct attribution. The analogy of channel capacity is useful not only in evaluating derivative works but also in guiding the creation of new works. By understanding the channel capacity, creators can ensure that their work falls within acceptable bounds of attribution.

To illustrate, consider a scenario where an author writes a blog post summarizing a complex academic paper. The goal is to convey the paper's key findings to a broader audience. Using information theory, we can analyze how much of the original paper's information is preserved in the blog post. The entropy of the original paper is likely high, given its complexity and detail. The blog post, being a summary, will have lower entropy. The mutual information between the paper and the blog post will indicate how much of the paper's information is actually conveyed in the summary. If the blog post simply rephrases the paper's abstract and conclusions, the mutual information will be relatively high. However, if the blog post provides new interpretations, contextualization, or critical analysis, the mutual information will be lower. The channel capacity analogy helps us understand the acceptable level of summarization. A good summary will transmit the key findings of the original paper without directly copying large sections of text. It will respect the channel capacity by adding its own unique contribution (analysis, explanation) while still acknowledging the source of the information. If the blog post fails to adequately attribute the original paper, or if it presents the paper's findings as its own original work, it could be seen as violating attribution principles, particularly if the mutual information is high, indicating a substantial reliance on the original paper's content.

The application of information theoretic bounds presents some inherent challenges. Estimating probabilities, calculating entropy, and determining mutual information can be computationally intensive, particularly with large and complex works. Also, defining appropriate thresholds for entropy and mutual information will require careful consideration of legal precedents, industry standards, and the specific context of each case. Despite these challenges, information theory offers a valuable framework for understanding and quantifying the complexities of attribution in the digital age. By providing a more objective and nuanced assessment of authorship, these bounds can contribute to a more fair and equitable distribution of credit in creative endeavors. It compels us to move beyond subjective judgements of similarity and embrace a more rigorous, data-driven approach to safeguarding author's production.

5.1 Entropy and Attribution Uncertainty

Entropy, in the context of attribution, serves as a measure of uncertainty or randomness associated with identifying the true author or originator of a work. It quantifies the lack of predictability in determining the source of a piece of content, especially when dealing with derivative works, collaborations, or situations where authorship is obscured or contested. High entropy implies a high degree of uncertainty, making attribution difficult, while low entropy suggests a clear and easily identifiable source. Consider a scenario where a song contains snippets of multiple existing tracks, remixed and altered to varying degrees. The higher the number of original sources and the more fragmented their use, the greater the entropy associated with attributing the final product to any single artist. This high entropy makes it incredibly challenging to determine the extent to which each artist contributed and, consequently, what portion of the final product can be attributed to each of them. Entropy alone doesn't provide specific attribution; rather, it highlights the complexity of the attribution task and guides the selection of appropriate analytical methods.

Attribution uncertainty, on the other hand, directly acknowledges the inherent limitations and potential errors in the process of assigning authorship. It reflects the degree of doubt or ambiguity that exists even after applying the best available attribution techniques. Uncertainty can arise from various sources, including incomplete data, methodological limitations, or the intentional obfuscation of authorship. It's crucial to recognize and quantify this uncertainty to provide a realistic assessment of attribution claims and avoid overstating the confidence in attribution results. Consider a scenario in scientific research where multiple authors contribute to a paper. While each author might be assigned specific sections, the integration of ideas and the iterative process of revision can make it challenging to precisely attribute each contribution. Moreover, the availability of funding and the prestige associated with the publication might incentivize some authors to overstate their contributions while downplaying those of others. This creates attribution uncertainty because the official authorship list might not accurately reflect the true intellectual contributions of each individual. Addressing this type of uncertainty requires careful consideration of qualitative data, such as personal communications, lab notebooks, and acknowledgments, alongside quantitative measures of contribution. Failing to account for such uncertainties can result in unfair attribution and can undermine the integrity of the scientific process.

The link between entropy and attribution uncertainty lies in the fact that high entropy generally leads to increased attribution uncertainty. When the source of a work is highly uncertain (high entropy), it becomes more difficult to confidently assign authorship, resulting in higher uncertainty in the attribution process. Conversely, low entropy typically leads to lower attribution uncertainty, as a clear and easily identifiable source makes attribution more straightforward. However, it's important to note that low entropy doesn't always guarantee low uncertainty. Even with a seemingly clear source, hidden complexities or intentional misrepresentation can still introduce uncertainty. For example, a document might appear to be written by a single author, but ghostwriting or extensive editing by others could create uncertainty about the true extent of their contribution.

To effectively manage entropy and reduce attribution uncertainty, several strategies can be employed. One approach is to utilize sophisticated analytical techniques to deconstruct complex works and identify their constituent elements. This might involve source code analysis for software, signal processing for audio recordings, or stylistic analysis for written text. By breaking down the work into smaller, more manageable components, it becomes easier to trace the origins of each component and attribute them to their respective sources. Another strategy is to incorporate contextual information into the attribution process. This includes examining the historical context in which the work was created, the relationships between potential authors, and any available documentation or metadata that might shed light on authorship. For instance, in the case of collaboratively written documents, tracking version control history and analyzing communication logs can provide valuable insights into the contributions of each author. Additionally, involving domain experts who are familiar with the subject matter and the relevant authorship practices can help to resolve ambiguities and reduce uncertainty. Consider a complex piece of musical composition which involves various musicians, producers, and engineers. Deciphering the individual contributions of each party requires not only technical analysis of the audio tracks, but also a thorough understanding of the recording process, the established roles within the music industry, and any existing agreements regarding authorship and royalties.

Furthermore, establishing clear and transparent authorship practices from the outset can significantly reduce entropy and uncertainty. This includes defining roles and responsibilities, documenting contributions, and implementing mechanisms for resolving authorship disputes. In collaborative projects, it's crucial to have a written agreement that outlines the criteria for authorship, the order of authors, and the process for handling conflicts. In organizational settings, implementing clear policies for intellectual property ownership and attribution can prevent disputes and ensure that contributors receive appropriate credit for their work. Consider academic research, where co-authorship disputes are frequent. Instituting a system for documenting each author's contributions to the research design, data collection, analysis, and writing can clarify roles and responsibilities. This reduces ambiguity, minimizes disputes, and ultimately enhances the integrity of the research process.

Ultimately, managing entropy and attribution uncertainty requires a combination of analytical techniques, contextual awareness, and proactive authorship practices. By acknowledging the inherent limitations in the attribution process and by employing strategies to reduce uncertainty, it's possible to provide a more accurate and fair assessment of authorship claims. This is especially critical in the digital age, where the ease of copying and modifying works has created new challenges for attribution and where the need for robust attribution frameworks is more pressing than ever. It is through a comprehensive approach that we can begin to navigate the complexities of authorship and ensure that creators receive the recognition and reward they deserve.

5.2 Mutual Information Measures

Attribution, at its core, concerns the relationship between an original work and its derivative counterparts. Traditional methods often rely on simple comparisons of textual similarity or identifying direct copies of specific elements. However, these approaches struggle to capture the nuances of transformative works, where ideas are reinterpreted, styles are emulated, or components are remixed. This is where mutual information measures come into play, offering a powerful lens for analyzing the statistical dependence between authored works. Mutual information, fundamentally, quantifies the amount of information that one random variable reveals about another. In the context of attribution, these random variables represent characteristics of the original work and its potential derivatives. For example, we might consider the distribution of word frequencies, the presence of specific stylistic features, or the arrangement of musical notes. If knowing something about these characteristics in the derivative work allows us to predict something about the original, then a degree of mutual information exists, suggesting a link between the two. This link, while not proving direct copying, provides evidence supporting or refuting a claim of authorship infringement. The larger the mutual information, the stronger the dependence, and the more likely it is that the derivative work is substantially based on the original.

Consider a scenario where a musician samples a short melody from an existing song and incorporates it into a new composition. A simple comparison of note sequences might identify the sampled section, but it wouldn't necessarily capture the extent to which the sample influenced the overall structure, harmonic progression, or emotional tone of the new work. Mutual information measures, on the other hand, could be used to assess the dependence between the melodic contours, rhythmic patterns, or even the timbral characteristics of the original and derivative compositions. If the new work exhibits a high degree of mutual information with respect to these features, it would suggest that the sampling had a significant impact on its overall design, even if the sample itself only constitutes a small portion of the final product. Moreover, calculating mutual information between the stylistic choices made in both songs, the musical keys, and the various instrumentations used would paint a clearer picture of possible plagiarism. It becomes possible to measure not just the presence of a copied element, but the presence of a creative fingerprint from the original artist to the work that is being scrutinized.

The practical application of mutual information measures requires careful consideration of several factors. First, it is crucial to select appropriate features that capture the essence of the original work and are relevant to the potential forms of derivative works. For textual analysis, this might involve using n-grams (sequences of n words), syntactic structures, or semantic representations. For musical analysis, features could include pitch contours, rhythmic patterns, chord progressions, or timbral characteristics. The choice of features should be guided by an understanding of the creative process and the ways in which authors typically build upon existing works. Second, it is important to address the challenges of data preprocessing and normalization. Raw data often contains noise and irrelevant variations that can obscure the underlying relationships between works. Techniques like stemming, lemmatization, and stop word removal can help to clean and standardize textual data. Similarly, musical data may require normalization of pitch, tempo, and dynamics to ensure that variations due to performance or recording quality do not distort the results. Third, calculating mutual information can be computationally intensive, especially when dealing with large datasets or complex features. Efficient algorithms and data structures are essential for making the process tractable. Furthermore, it's important to choose an appropriate estimator for mutual information, as different estimators have different biases and variances, particularly when dealing with limited data.

Beyond simply quantifying the degree of dependence between works, mutual information measures can also be used to establish attribution bounds. By setting a threshold on the amount of mutual information that is considered acceptable, we can define a boundary between legitimate derivative works and those that infringe upon the original author's rights. This threshold should be determined based on a careful balancing of competing interests, taking into account factors such as the purpose and character of the derivative work, the nature of the original work, and the potential impact on the market for the original. Imagine, for example, setting a mutual information threshold for derivative artworks based on an original photograph. If a new artwork exhibits mutual information above the threshold with the photograph, it might be considered an unauthorized derivative, triggering copyright concerns. Conversely, if the mutual information falls below the threshold, it might be deemed a transformative work that falls within the bounds of fair use. This approach provides a more objective and data-driven way to assess attribution claims, reducing the subjectivity and uncertainty that often plague traditional methods.

However, the use of mutual information measures in attribution is not without its limitations. One key challenge is the interpretation of results. While mutual information can quantify the degree of statistical dependence between works, it does not necessarily imply causation or intentional copying. A high degree of mutual information could arise due to independent creation, common influences, or random chance. Therefore, it is crucial to consider the context surrounding the works and to examine other evidence, such as authorial intent, access to the original work, and similarities in specific creative choices. Moreover, mutual information measures are sensitive to the choice of features and parameters. Different features may capture different aspects of the works, and different parameter settings can lead to different results. It is important to carefully validate the results and to consider the potential biases introduced by the choice of features and parameters. A thorough analysis should involve experimenting with different features and parameter settings to assess the robustness of the findings.

In conclusion, mutual information measures offer a powerful and versatile tool for assessing attribution in the digital age. By quantifying the statistical dependence between original works and their derivatives, they provide a more objective and data-driven way to evaluate attribution claims. While not a silver bullet, mutual information measures can be a valuable addition to the toolkit of authors, legal professionals, and policymakers seeking to protect intellectual property rights and foster creativity in the digital environment. Careful consideration of the limitations and appropriate interpretation of results are essential for ensuring that these measures are used effectively and ethically. In the end, mutual information measures help shift the analysis of authorship from subjective impressions to measurable dependencies, providing a strong technical foundation for protecting authors' rights. The goal is not simply to detect copying, but to fairly assess the influence and contribution of original works in the creation of new ones.

5.3 Channel Capacity and Bounds

Our ability to discern the origin of a piece of information, a creative work, or an intellectual property has become inextricably linked to the sophisticated tools we wield in the digital age. Yet, this very sophistication introduces a critical question: how much information can be legitimately extracted from an original work before it infringes upon the author's rights? The answer lies, at least in part, within the realm of information theory, specifically the concept of channel capacity and its application in establishing rigorous attribution bounds.

Think of the original authored work as a signal transmitted through a noisy channel. This channel represents the processes of modification, adaptation, or derivation that the work undergoes. The recipient, in this analogy, is the derivative work, carrying a portion of the original signal, potentially altered or obscured by noise. The channel capacity, in this context, defines the maximum rate at which information from the original work can be reliably transmitted to the derivative work without losing the essence of its attribution. It is this concept of "reliable transmission" that is key to establishing attribution bounds. If the information transfer rate exceeds the channel capacity, the derivative work becomes so dissimilar that attributing its origins becomes increasingly challenging and, crucially, less justifiable.

The power of channel capacity lies in its ability to provide a quantifiable metric for assessing the degree of dependence between the original and the derivative work. Imagine a painter who takes inspiration from another artist and tries to emulate them, it will change the output as much as possible to don't get sued. Applying the Shannon capacity to the context of authorship and copyright would be quite complex, but let's think about it as the rate at which the message (e.g. information) is encoded and transmitted through a channel, so it is possible to analyze how much of a copyrighted creation has been transmitted to the new one without breaching any attribution law.

To apply information-theoretic bounds, we need to quantify the information content of both the original and derivative works. This is where entropy, a fundamental concept in information theory, comes into play. Entropy measures the uncertainty or randomness associated with a variable. In the context of attribution, we can use entropy to quantify the uncertainty surrounding the authorship of a derivative work. A high entropy in the derivative work might indicate a significant departure from the original, whereas low entropy could suggest a strong dependence.

Mutual information provides a powerful tool for quantifying the shared information between the original and derivative works. It measures the reduction in uncertainty about one variable given knowledge of the other. High mutual information implies a strong dependence, suggesting that the derivative work relies heavily on the original. Conversely, low mutual information suggests a weak dependence, potentially indicating that the derivative work has significantly diverged from its source. Calculating the mutual information between the original work and its derivative allows us to establish a quantitative measure of their relationship, which can then be compared to predefined bounds to assess the legitimacy of attribution. We can also use Kullback Leibler divergence to measure the difference between the probability distributions to try to understand how much the authorship of the new creative asset is diverging.

Let's consider a musical composition. The original song represents the input signal, and a remix represents the output. The remixer, in this context, is essentially encoding the original song into a new format. If the remix preserves the core melody, harmony, and rhythm of the original, the channel capacity is high, and the attribution is clear. However, if the remix significantly alters these elements, adding substantial new material and obscuring the original's essence, the channel capacity decreases, and the attribution becomes less clear. This scenario helps illustrate how information-theoretic bounds can provide a framework for evaluating the degree to which a remix infringes upon the copyright of the original composition. This idea can be extended to a lot of other fields: consider a scientific article being cited, a code library being copied, or a painting being referenced.

Attribution bounds based on channel capacity also provide a mechanism for balancing the rights of original authors with the need for creativity and innovation. By setting a threshold on the maximum amount of information that can be extracted from a work without violating attribution principles, we can encourage derivative works that build upon existing knowledge while respecting the rights of the original creators. This balance is crucial for fostering a vibrant and dynamic creative ecosystem. Moreover, channel capacity provides a framework for assessing the potential harm caused by unauthorized use of copyrighted material. By quantifying the amount of information extracted from the original work, we can estimate the economic value lost by the copyright holder, which can be used to determine appropriate remedies in cases of infringement.

However, applying information-theoretic concepts to attribution is not without its challenges. Quantifying the information content of creative works can be subjective and context-dependent. The choice of appropriate entropy measures and the definition of relevant variables require careful consideration. Furthermore, the computational complexity of calculating mutual information can be significant, particularly for large-scale datasets. Consider how copyright infringements can be hard to prove when the infringed work isn't distributed or is slightly different, using information-theoretic bounds can help in these specific scenarios. To address these challenges, we need to develop robust and efficient algorithms for information extraction and analysis. We also need to establish standardized metrics for quantifying information content and defining appropriate bounds. These efforts will require collaboration between researchers from various disciplines, including information theory, computer science, law, and the humanities.

Looking ahead, the use of information-theoretic bounds in

attribution is likely to become increasingly important in the digital age. As creative works become more complex and collaborative, the need for robust and objective measures of attribution will grow. By embracing the principles of information theory, we can develop frameworks that protect the rights of authors while fostering innovation and creativity. Furthermore, the use of information-theoretic bounds can help to promote transparency and accountability in the digital marketplace. By providing clear and objective measures of attribution, we can empower creators to protect their work and ensure that they receive proper recognition for their contributions. This, in turn, will foster a more equitable and sustainable ecosystem for creative production.

Ultimately, establishing clear and defensible bounds on the use of copyrighted material is essential for protecting the rights of creators and fostering innovation. Channel capacity, as a tool within information theory, offers a rigorous and quantifiable framework for achieving this balance, paving the way for a more just and equitable digital world. It is a new approach to protect the rights of copyright holders, it helps to understand and measure a copy using the tools and techniques of information theory and math. This approach it is becoming more relevant with the recent advances in AI and automation because it creates an objective metric to understand who produced what.

6 Chapter 6: Practical Applications of Bounds

Attribution bounds, though conceptually elegant, gain their true value when translated into practical applications. The theoretical frameworks, the statistical models, and the information-theoretic approaches discussed in previous chapters all serve the ultimate purpose of safeguarding authors' production in a tangible way. This chapter will delve into the actionable strategies and real-world scenarios where these bounds can be effectively employed.

The art world, both digital and traditional, faces constant threats to its integrity. From unauthorized reproductions to blatant copies sold as originals, artistic works are prime targets for infringement. Attribution bounds offer a powerful tool for protecting artists' rights. Consider a painter whose work is digitally scanned and manipulated to create a derivative piece. By establishing a clear bound on the permissible degree of alteration, we can determine whether the derivative work infringes upon the original artist's attribution rights. For example, if the derivative work retains a high degree of visual similarity to the original, exceeding a predefined threshold based on feature extraction and comparison, it could be deemed a violation of the artist's rights. This threshold could be determined statistically, based on an analysis of the artist's style and the typical variations within their body of work. This also requires a system of registration, such as embedding digital watermarks or cryptographic signatures, so that the authorship and original integrity can be verified. The system could analyze metadata to determine authorship but also could analyze the image data to assess the provenance of the product through file analysis, camera identification, and other methods. It is essential to know the details of the software, hardware, and other tools used to create the artwork to assess originality. Digital forensics must therefore be used to analyze the software. Consider a sculpture which has been copied and sold in an online auction, this situation can be detected through visual comparison and a violation of the attribution of the author can be proved in a courtroom, this situation could also be detected using techniques from statistical analysis, Bayesian approaches and entropy. The bounds act as a quantifiable measure of similarity and difference, assisting legal experts in determining infringement.

Fair use, a cornerstone of copyright law, permits the limited use of copyrighted material without permission from the copyright holder. However, determining what constitutes "fair" use is often a complex and subjective process. Attribution bounds provide a framework for making more objective assessments. Imagine a film critic incorporating snippets from a movie into a review. The question becomes: how much of the original movie can be used before the critic's work infringes on the filmmaker's copyright? Information-theoretic bounds can be particularly helpful here. By quantifying the amount of information extracted from the movie and used in the review, we can assess whether the use falls within acceptable limits. If the information extracted is minimal and serves primarily to illustrate the critic's points, it's more likely to be considered fair use. Conversely, if the review heavily relies on the movie's plot, characters, or dialogue, exceeding the established information bound, it may constitute copyright infringement. Moreover, the nature of the transformative work matters. If the critic adds substantial commentary, analysis, and critique, the use is more likely to be considered fair. Attribution bounds must, therefore, consider the transformative aspects of the derivative work, not just the quantity of material used. A legal expert could use the tools to assist in these types of decisions, or a machine learning model could be constructed to provide a recommendation. These tools could be used by content creators to prevent them from crossing the line into infringement. Therefore the content creator would not need to hire a lawyer until they are already in a legal battle.

Plagiarism, the act of presenting someone else's work as your own, is a pervasive problem across academic, professional, and creative domains. Attribution bounds offer innovative strategies for detecting and combating plagiarism. Traditional plagiarism detection tools primarily rely on identifying exact matches or near-identical phrases between a submitted work and a database of existing texts. While effective in many cases, these tools often fail to detect more sophisticated forms of plagiarism, such as paraphrasing or subtle rewrites. Statistical attribution bounds can address this limitation. By analyzing the statistical properties of an author's writing style—such as word choice, sentence structure, and grammatical patterns—we can create a unique "fingerprint" for their work. This fingerprint can then be compared against other texts to identify instances where the author's style has been replicated without proper attribution, even if the words themselves have been altered. Furthermore, causal inference techniques can be employed to investigate the source of plagiarized content. By examining the chain of modifications and influences that led to the plagiarized work, we can trace its origins back to the original source, even if the plagiarist has attempted to obscure their tracks. The bounds help educational institutions and employers maintain academic integrity and ethical standards, or could be used to provide a detection service which could be monetized. This could be used to prevent fraud or to ensure quality in creative, artistic and academic products.

Beyond these specific applications, attribution bounds can also inform the development of broader policies and guidelines for the use of digital content. For example, online platforms can use attribution bounds to create rules governing the remixing and sharing of user-generated content. By setting clear limits on the permissible degree of modification and reuse, these platforms can foster a culture of responsible innovation while respecting the rights of content creators. Another application can be found in content generation. This process is used to create a vast amount of content every day, and the copyright laws that govern content generation are not yet decided. However, attribution bounds can be used to ensure that the new content does not violate copyright laws. For example, if a content generator uses existing content as a base, the attribution bounds can be used to ensure that the generated content does not violate copyright laws. This could be used to create new content without violating any laws, and could be used to improve the quality of the content. Attribution bounds can also guide the development of more effective copyright licensing schemes. Rather than relying on blanket licenses that grant or deny all rights, attribution bounds allow for more granular control over the use of copyrighted material. Authors can specify the precise limits of permissible use, allowing others to build upon their work while ensuring that they receive proper credit and compensation.

In essence, the practical applications of attribution bounds are vast and varied. By providing a framework for quantifying and enforcing authorship rights, these bounds empower creators to protect their work, foster responsible innovation, and navigate the complex landscape of digital production. However, their effectiveness depends on careful implementation, ongoing refinement, and a commitment to balancing the rights of authors with the needs of society. Consider, for instance, the challenges of applying attribution bounds to collaborative works. When multiple authors contribute to a single project, determining the relative contributions of each individual and establishing appropriate attribution can be complex. Attribution bounds can help by providing a framework for quantifying the individual contributions of each author, based on metrics such as the amount of code written, the number of ideas contributed, or the extent of editing performed. This information can then be used to generate a more accurate and equitable attribution statement.

These frameworks offer tangible solutions to protect and acknowledge authorship in an increasingly complex digital landscape. Their adaptability across various domains underscores their potential to shape a future where creativity is both encouraged and safeguarded.

6.1 Protecting Artistic Works

Protecting artistic works in the digital age requires a multifaceted approach, moving beyond traditional copyright mechanisms to incorporate proactive strategies and adaptable frameworks. The very nature of digital art, with its ease of reproduction and modification, demands that artists and legal professionals understand and implement attribution bounds to safeguard their creations effectively. Therefore, let's first delve into understanding the specific challenges digital artists face and then explore the practical steps to mitigate these risks, ensuring the attribution of their artistic endeavors.

The digital landscape is fraught with challenges that make protecting artistic works significantly harder than ever before. Unauthorized reproduction is rampant, with art readily copied and distributed without permission. Modifications occur with alarming frequency, often without the original artist's consent or even knowledge. Attribution is routinely omitted or misrepresented, particularly in online contexts where anonymity is common. Derivative works may be created and commercially exploited without proper licensing or credit. Moreover, the global reach of the internet complicates enforcement, as copyright laws vary significantly across jurisdictions. These factors underscore the need for a robust and adaptable strategy for protecting artistic works in the digital age. To be effective in our pursuits, we must ensure, as creators, that the legal rights surrounding our artistic expressions remain solid and unassailable.

One essential aspect of safeguarding an artist's works is a clear and well-defined license agreement. This agreement should specify precisely how the work can be used, modified, and distributed. It must address issues such as commercial use, derivative works, and attribution requirements. Creative Commons licenses provide a useful starting point, offering a range of options from "Attribution Only" to "Non-Commercial, No Derivatives." However, artists should consider customizing these licenses to fit their specific needs and preferences. A carefully drafted license agreement provides a legal basis for enforcing attribution rights and preventing unauthorized use. It is important for artists to obtain legal advice when drafting or modifying license agreements to ensure that their rights are adequately protected.

In addition to licensing, proactive monitoring is essential for detecting and addressing unauthorized use. Implement tools to scour the internet for instances of your work being used without permission. Reverse image search is one simple yet powerful tool. Services such as Google Images and TinEye allow you to upload an image and find websites where that image appears. This can help identify cases of unauthorized reproduction or modification. Watermarking involves embedding a subtle identifier within the artwork itself. Digital watermarks can be resistant to removal and can provide evidence of ownership and attribution. Regularly checking social media, online marketplaces, and art-sharing platforms is also a necessary step. These platforms are often breeding grounds for copyright infringement, and early detection is crucial for minimizing damage.

When unauthorized use is detected, taking swift and decisive action is critical. The first step is usually to send a "cease and desist" letter to the infringing party. This letter should clearly identify the copyrighted work, the infringing use, and the demand for immediate cessation. It should also state the consequences of non-compliance, such as legal action. In many cases, a cease and desist letter is enough to resolve the issue. However, if the infringement continues, legal action may be necessary. This could involve filing a copyright infringement lawsuit, which can be costly and time-consuming, but may be the only way to protect your rights. Consider alternative dispute resolution methods, such as mediation or arbitration, before resorting to litigation. These methods can often be more efficient and cost-effective.

Attribution is a moral imperative, a professional courtesy, and a legal requirement. Digital creators need to actively embed attribution information into their works. Metadata is a powerful tool for embedding information about the artist, copyright owner, and licensing terms directly into the digital file. Most image editing software allows you to add metadata to your files, including information such as the artist's name, contact information, and copyright notice. This metadata can be read by software and websites, ensuring that the attribution information travels with the artwork. Watermarks, while often used for copyright protection, can also serve as a form of attribution. Consider incorporating your name or logo into the watermark itself. When sharing your work online, always include a clear and prominent attribution statement. This statement should include your name, the title of the work, and any relevant licensing information.

Fair Use and Copyright laws are intricate and often misunderstood. Understanding the nuances of these laws is essential for artists and legal professionals alike. Fair use allows the use of copyrighted material without permission for certain purposes, such as criticism, commentary, news reporting, teaching, scholarship, and research. However, the application of fair use is highly fact-specific and depends on a four-factor test: the purpose and character of the use, the nature of the copyrighted work, the amount and substantiality of the portion used, and the effect of the use on the potential market for the copyrighted work. Artists should seek legal advice when determining whether their use of copyrighted material qualifies as fair use. Copyright law protects original works of authorship, including literary, dramatic, musical, and certain other intellectual works. Copyright protection arises automatically upon creation of the work and lasts for the life of the author plus 70 years. Registering your copyright with the U.S. Copyright Office provides additional legal benefits, such as the ability to sue for statutory damages and attorney's fees in copyright infringement cases.

Ultimately, protecting artistic works in the digital age requires a combination of legal strategies, technological tools, and proactive monitoring. Artists must take steps to secure their rights by licensing their works carefully, embedding attribution information, and actively monitoring for unauthorized use. When infringement is detected, they must act swiftly and decisively to enforce their rights. By understanding and implementing attribution bounds, artists can safeguard their creations and ensure that their contributions are properly recognized and rewarded. This comprehensive approach protects their artistic integrity and promotes a culture of respect for intellectual property in the digital world.

6.2 Fair Use and Copyright

Fair use represents a crucial balancing act within copyright law, permitting limited use of copyrighted material without needing permission from the rights holder. It is not a loophole or an exception, but rather an integral aspect of copyright designed to foster creativity, scholarship, education, and commentary. The doctrine aims to reconcile the author's right to control their work with the public's interest in accessing and building upon existing knowledge and culture. Navigating fair use, however, can feel like traversing a minefield, especially for beginners. Many creators find themselves bewildered by its subjective nature and the lack of definitive rules. To effectively utilize fair use, you must grasp its underlying principles and how they are applied in practice.

At its core, fair use assessment hinges on a four-factor test, as outlined in Section 107 of the Copyright Act. These factors serve as guidelines, rather than rigid rules, and their relative weight can vary depending on the specific circumstances. The first factor concerns the purpose and character of the use, including whether such use is of a commercial nature or is for nonprofit educational purposes. Transformative use, where the original work is altered with new expression, meaning, or message, weighs heavily in favor of fair use. Parody, criticism, commentary, news reporting, teaching, scholarship, and research are all examples of purposes that often support a fair use claim. The more transformative your use, the less important the other factors become. Therefore, simply reproducing a work verbatim, even for educational purposes, is less likely to be considered fair use than using a small portion of it to critique or analyze the original.

The second factor considers the nature of the copyrighted work. This addresses the characteristics of the work being used. Courts generally grant wider latitude for uses of factual works compared to highly creative or fictional works. This is because copyright protection is stronger for original works of artistic expression than for works primarily based on facts or information. Furthermore, whether the work is published or unpublished also matters. Using unpublished works is generally disfavored under fair use principles because the author retains a greater right to control the first public dissemination of their work.

The third factor examines the amount and substantiality of the portion used in relation to the copyrighted work as a whole. This assesses not only the quantity of the material taken, but also its qualitative significance. Even if you only use a small portion of a work, if that portion is the "heart" of the work – the most recognizable or essential element – it can weigh against fair use. There are no fixed percentages or word counts that automatically qualify as fair use. Instead, courts look at whether the amount taken was necessary for the purpose of the use. For instance, a film critic may need to show excerpts of a movie to illustrate their points, while a scholar might need to quote passages from a book to support their analysis. The key is to use only as much as is needed to achieve your purpose.

Finally, the fourth factor evaluates the effect of the use upon the potential market for or value of the copyrighted work. This is often considered the most important factor, as it focuses on the economic harm that the use might inflict on the copyright holder. If your use of the copyrighted material serves as a substitute for the original, thereby diminishing its market value, it will likely weigh heavily against fair use. This doesn't necessarily mean that any commercial use is automatically unfair.

Rather, the question is whether your use is competing with the original work or fulfilling a different market need. A parody, for example, might be a commercial venture, but it is unlikely to be seen as a substitute for the original work being parodied. Understanding these factors is just the first step. Applying them in practice requires careful analysis and judgment. It is always prudent to err on the side of caution and seek legal advice if you are unsure whether your use qualifies as fair. Keep detailed records of your reasoning for claiming fair use, documenting how each of the four factors applies to your situation. This documentation can be invaluable if you are ever challenged in court. Remember, fair use is a fact-specific determination, and the outcome of any particular case will depend on the unique circumstances.

Beyond the four-factor test, several additional considerations can influence a fair use determination. The nature of your audience can be relevant. Uses that primarily benefit the public, such as educational materials or news reporting, are more likely to be considered fair use than uses that solely benefit private individuals or commercial entities. Your good faith in claiming fair use can also be a factor. If you have made a genuine effort to understand and apply the fair use principles, this can strengthen your case, even if a court ultimately disagrees with your assessment.

Fair use is not a one-time decision. It is an ongoing process that requires you to revisit your assessment as your project evolves. If you make significant changes to your use of copyrighted material, you should re-evaluate whether your claim of fair use still holds up. Similarly, if new case law emerges that clarifies or alters the interpretation of fair use principles, you should take those developments into account. It's crucial to understand that fair use is an affirmative defense, meaning that the burden is on you to prove that your use is fair. The copyright holder does not have to prove that your use is infringing; you must demonstrate that it is justified under the fair use doctrine. This underscores the importance of thorough documentation and careful analysis.

Finally, keep in mind that fair use laws vary from country to country. What constitutes fair use in the United States may not be considered fair dealing (the equivalent concept in some other jurisdictions) elsewhere. If you are distributing your work internationally, you need to be aware of the applicable copyright laws in each country. In conclusion, fair use is a complex and nuanced area of copyright law. While the four-factor test provides a framework for analysis, it is not a substitute for careful judgment and legal expertise. By understanding the principles of fair use and applying them thoughtfully, you can navigate the legal landscape and create works that are both innovative and respectful of copyright law. My personal journey through copyright law has taught me that diligence and a deep understanding of these principles are essential for anyone working with creative content.

6.3 Combating Plagiarism

Combating Plagiarism

The specter of plagiarism haunts creators, educators, and institutions alike, demanding rigorous strategies for prevention, detection, and remediation. It's not simply about copying and pasting; plagiarism encompasses a spectrum of offenses, from verbatim replication without attribution to subtler forms like paraphrasing too closely or submitting someone else's ideas as one's own. It undermines the principles of academic integrity, devalues original thought, and potentially carries significant legal and professional ramifications. Thus, a multifaceted approach is crucial, integrating technological tools with educational initiatives and clear institutional policies.

Let's begin with prevention, and the pivotal role education plays here. Plagiarism, at its root, often stems from a lack of understanding of proper citation practices and the nuances of academic writing. Students, particularly those new to higher education, may not fully grasp the importance of giving credit where it's due or the permissible limits of paraphrasing. Therefore, comprehensive instruction on citation styles (MLA, APA, Chicago, etc.), paraphrasing techniques, and the ethical implications of plagiarism is paramount. This should be embedded within the curriculum, not treated as a one-off workshop. Instructors should explicitly model proper citation practices in their own work and provide ample opportunities for students to practice and receive feedback on their source integration skills. Furthermore, emphasizing the value of original thought and critical analysis can encourage students to engage with sources in a more meaningful way, reducing the temptation to simply copy or paraphrase. Assignment design also matters; tasks that encourage critical thinking, analysis, and the synthesis of multiple sources are less susceptible to plagiarism than those that simply require regurgitation of information. Instead of asking students to summarize existing research, consider asking them to analyze it, compare and contrast different perspectives, or apply it to a novel scenario. Finally, clear communication of expectations and consequences is essential. Institutional policies on plagiarism should be readily accessible and clearly articulated, outlining the various forms of plagiarism and the disciplinary actions that will be taken in response.

Now, let's transition to the technological tools available for plagiarism detection. A multitude of software programs, such as Turnitin, SafeAssign, and iThenticate, can analyze submitted texts and compare them against vast databases of online content, academic papers, and previously submitted student work. These tools highlight potential instances of plagiarism, providing instructors with a valuable starting point for investigation. However, it's crucial to remember that these programs are not infallible. They identify similarities, not necessarily intentional plagiarism. A high similarity score does not automatically equate to academic dishonesty; it could indicate proper use of quotations with incorrect attribution, or common knowledge expressed in a similar way. Therefore, instructors must carefully review the reports generated by these tools, considering the context of the detected similarities and the student's overall understanding of the material. Over-reliance on these tools without critical judgment can lead to false accusations and erode trust between students and instructors. Some best practices when deploying these tools include calibrating the sensitivity settings appropriately and informing students about their use beforehand. This transparency can serve as a deterrent and provide students with an opportunity to clarify any potential issues proactively. Furthermore, institutions should invest in training for faculty on how to effectively use and interpret the results generated by these tools.

However, technology and education alone cannot fully address the issue; robust institutional policies and procedures are equally critical. A comprehensive plagiarism policy should clearly define plagiarism, outlining the various forms it can take and the consequences for each. It should also establish a clear process for investigating suspected cases of plagiarism, ensuring fairness and due process for all parties involved. This process should include opportunities for the student to respond to the allegations, present evidence, and appeal the decision. The severity of the consequences should be commensurate with the severity of the offense, ranging from a warning or a failing grade on the assignment to suspension or expulsion from the institution. Consistency in the application of the policy is crucial to maintain fairness and deter future violations. Furthermore, institutions should provide support services for students who have been accused of plagiarism, such as academic advising and counseling. Addressing the underlying causes of plagiarism, whether it's a lack of understanding, poor time management, or academic pressure, can help prevent future occurrences.

Let's consider the role of the internet and online resources and how they've revolutionized access to information, they have also exacerbated the problem of plagiarism. The ease with which students can copy and paste content from websites has made it more tempting than ever to engage in academic dishonesty. Moreover, the proliferation of online paper mills and essay writing services provides students with ready-made solutions to their assignments, further undermining the principles of academic integrity. To combat these challenges, institutions need to adapt their plagiarism detection strategies to account for the evolving online landscape. This includes utilizing software that can identify content from online paper mills and educating students about the ethical implications of using these services. Additionally, instructors can design assignments that require students to engage with online sources in a critical and analytical way, rather than simply copying and pasting information. Requiring students to evaluate the credibility and bias of online sources, for example, can help them develop the critical thinking skills necessary to avoid plagiarism. Promoting a culture of academic integrity online is also essential. This includes encouraging students to report instances of plagiarism they observe and fostering a sense of shared responsibility for upholding academic standards.

Now, let's turn to the important area of paraphrasing and the subtle, yet significant, distinctions between legitimate paraphrasing and plagiarism. While paraphrasing is a valuable skill for integrating sources into one's own writing, it can easily cross the line into plagiarism if not done properly. A legitimate paraphrase restates the original source's ideas in one's own words and sentence structure, while still accurately representing the original meaning. It also requires proper attribution to the original source. Plagiarism, on the other hand, occurs when a paraphrase is too close to the original source in terms of wording or sentence structure, even if attribution is provided. To avoid this, students should strive to understand the original source's ideas thoroughly before attempting to paraphrase. They should then close the original source and try to restate the ideas from memory, focusing on capturing the essence of the argument rather than simply rearranging the words. Comparing the paraphrase to the original source to ensure that it is sufficiently different is also crucial. If the paraphrase is too close to the original, it should be revised.

Finally, combating plagiarism requires a collaborative effort from all stakeholders: students, instructors, institutions, and even technology providers. By working together, we can create a culture of academic integrity that values original thought, promotes responsible scholarship, and safeguards the integrity of the academic enterprise. This requires a shift in focus from simply detecting and punishing plagiarism to preventing it in the first place through education, support, and clear expectations. It also requires a willingness to adapt our strategies to meet the evolving challenges of the digital age.

7 Chapter 7: Future Directions & Challenges

The realm of authorship and attribution is not static; it's a constantly shifting landscape molded by technological advances, evolving societal norms, and increasingly complex collaborative dynamics. Predicting the future with certainty is impossible, but we can identify key trends and challenges that will likely shape the discourse around attribution bounds in the coming years. One prominent trend is the increasing interconnectedness of creative endeavors. Collaboration is no longer confined to geographically proximate individuals or even teams within a single organization. Global collaborations spanning multiple disciplines are becoming increasingly commonplace, requiring sophisticated attribution models capable of accurately reflecting the contributions of diverse participants. These models must move beyond simple source code attribution and consider the often subtle, yet crucial, contributions made in design, ideation, and conceptualization. This complexity is further amplified by the rise of open-source projects and creative commons licensing, which allow for the reuse and modification of existing works under specific conditions. Properly attributing these uses while maintaining the integrity of the original author's rights presents a significant challenge. We are moving towards a world where understanding the nuanced interplay of contributions becomes paramount to ensuring fair and accurate attribution.

Another significant challenge lies in the evolving definition of authorship itself. Traditionally, authorship has been closely tied to human creativity and intentionality. However, as technology becomes more sophisticated, it blurs these lines. Consider the scenario of a machine learning algorithm trained on a dataset of existing musical compositions, which then generates a novel piece of music. Who is the author? Is it the programmer who designed the algorithm? Is it the individual who curated the training dataset? Or is it the algorithm itself? This question necessitates a re-evaluation of the fundamental principles of authorship and the criteria for determining originality and creative contribution. Legal frameworks must adapt to address these new realities, potentially incorporating concepts like "algorithmic authorship" or establishing clear guidelines for the attribution of works created with the assistance of technology. The focus should be on developing frameworks that acknowledge the role of technology while upholding the rights and recognition of human contributors. Furthermore, the ethical implications of such automated creation need careful consideration. Should algorithms be granted the same rights and protections as human authors? How can we prevent bias and discrimination in algorithmically generated works? These questions demand thoughtful analysis and open dialogue to ensure that technological advancements do not undermine the principles of fairness and equity in the creative sphere.

Moreover, the increasing sophistication of techniques for manipulating and obscuring authorship information poses a serious threat. Digital watermarks can be removed, metadata can be altered, and even the stylistic fingerprint of an author can be mimicked. This necessitates the development of more robust and resilient attribution techniques that are resistant to tampering and capable of verifying authorship even in the face of deliberate obfuscation. Blockchain technology offers a promising avenue for establishing immutable records of authorship and provenance, but it is not without its challenges. Scalability, privacy concerns, and the need for widespread adoption are all hurdles that must be overcome. Furthermore, the legal admissibility of blockchain-based attribution records remains an open question in many jurisdictions. Beyond technological solutions, there is a need for increased awareness and education among creators, consumers, and legal professionals regarding the importance of accurate attribution and the methods for detecting and preventing authorship manipulation. The fight against plagiarism and copyright infringement requires a multi-faceted approach that combines technological innovation with legal and ethical frameworks.

Ethical considerations surrounding attribution are also becoming increasingly prominent. Attribution is not simply a matter of legal compliance; it is also a matter of fairness, respect, and recognition. Failure to properly attribute the work of others can have significant consequences, both for the individual author and for the broader creative community. It can undermine trust, discourage collaboration, and stifle innovation. Furthermore, there is a growing awareness of the potential for bias in attribution models. If an attribution model is trained on a dataset that is not representative of the broader creative landscape, it may systematically undervalue the contributions of certain groups or individuals. This is particularly concerning in the context of diversity and inclusion. Attribution models should be carefully designed and evaluated to ensure that they are fair, equitable, and transparent. This includes addressing issues of algorithmic bias and promoting the use of diverse datasets in the training process. Moreover, it is important to recognize that attribution is not always a zero-sum game. In many collaborative projects, multiple authors may contribute significantly to the final product. Attribution models should be designed to acknowledge and reward these contributions in a way that is both fair and motivating.

Looking ahead, the development of adaptive attribution frameworks will be crucial. These frameworks should be capable of dynamically adjusting to the specific context of a creative work, taking into account factors such as the type of work, the nature of the collaboration, and the applicable legal and ethical considerations. This requires a flexible and modular approach to attribution, allowing for the customization of attribution models to meet the unique needs of different creative communities. For instance, the attribution model used for a scientific publication may differ significantly from the model used for a work of visual art. Furthermore, adaptive attribution frameworks should be designed to evolve over time, incorporating new technological advancements and adapting to changing societal norms. This requires a continuous process of research, development, and evaluation, involving input from creators, consumers, legal professionals, and technology experts. Only through a collaborative and interdisciplinary approach can we hope to create attribution frameworks that are both effective and equitable in the face of the ever-evolving creative landscape.

In closing, the future of attribution is complex and uncertain, but it is also full of opportunities. By embracing innovation, addressing ethical considerations, and fostering collaboration, we can create a world where authorship is valued, creativity is encouraged, and the rights of all creators are protected. The ongoing development of attribution bounds serves as a crucial tool in navigating this complex terrain, ensuring that the principles of fairness, transparency, and accountability remain at the forefront of the creative process. It is incumbent upon us to continue pushing the boundaries of our understanding and to develop innovative solutions that meet the challenges of the digital age. Only then can we hope to create a truly sustainable and equitable creative ecosystem for future generations. The journey ahead is not without its obstacles, but with dedication, innovation, and a commitment to ethical principles, we can ensure that attribution remains a cornerstone of the creative process for years to come. The pursuit of fair and accurate attribution is not just a legal or technical challenge; it is a fundamental imperative for a thriving and equitable creative society. Let us embrace this challenge and work together to build a future where authorship is valued, creativity is celebrated, and the rights of all creators are respected.

7.1 Evolving Attribution Landscapes

The future of attribution isn't a linear projection of the present; it's a landscape undergoing tectonic shifts, driven by technological advancements, evolving social norms, and increasingly complex creative ecosystems. We must acknowledge the core principles that have guided attribution for decades, but also be ready to adapt those principles to circumstances that seem almost alien compared to the world in which they were formulated. A key challenge lies in bridging the gap between traditional legal frameworks, often designed for tangible works and individual authorship, and the fluid, collaborative, and increasingly automated world of digital content creation.

The rise of collaborative platforms and open-source movements has already complicated the notion of individual authorship. Large-scale projects, involving hundreds or even thousands of contributors, present a formidable challenge for traditional attribution mechanisms. How do we fairly credit each participant when their contributions range from writing a single line of code to designing a critical component of a complex system? Existing copyright laws are often inadequate for addressing these scenarios, as they tend to focus on clear-cut ownership and distinct authorship roles. Moving forward, we need attribution models that can accurately reflect the diverse contributions of each collaborator, potentially through tiered systems that acknowledge different levels of involvement and impact. Smart contracts and blockchain technology offer promising avenues for automating and transparently managing attribution in these collaborative environments, ensuring that each contributor receives due credit and potentially even royalties based on their contributions.

However, collaboration isn't the only factor reshaping the attribution landscape. The increasing sophistication of content creation tools is also blurring the lines of authorship. Consider scenarios where algorithms assist in generating text, music, or visual art. While the final product may bear the mark of a human artist, the underlying technology plays a significant role in shaping its form and content. Determining the appropriate level of attribution for the algorithm's creators and developers is a complex issue. Should they be considered co-authors, or should their contribution be acknowledged in a different way, perhaps through a disclaimer or a metadata tag? The answer likely lies somewhere in the middle, requiring a nuanced assessment of the algorithm's creative input and the extent to which it shaped the final work. This assessment may involve technical analysis to quantify the algorithm's contribution, as well as legal interpretation to determine its impact on authorship.

Ethical considerations are also coming to the forefront of the attribution debate. As attribution systems become more sophisticated and data-driven, there is a risk of perpetuating existing biases and inequalities. Algorithms trained on biased datasets may systematically under-attribute the contributions of certain individuals or groups, leading to unfair or inaccurate representations of authorship. For example, if an attribution model is trained primarily on data from Western cultures, it may fail to adequately recognize the contributions of artists or writers from other cultural backgrounds. Mitigating these biases requires careful attention to data collection and model design, as well as ongoing monitoring and evaluation to ensure fairness and equity. This means actively seeking diverse perspectives and incorporating them into the development of attribution systems, as well as being transparent about the limitations of these systems and their potential for bias.

Another critical area that needs attention is the development of standards and protocols for digital content provenance. Establishing a clear and verifiable chain of custody for digital works is essential for ensuring accurate attribution and preventing fraud. This involves developing technologies that can track the origin of a piece of content, as well as all subsequent modifications and uses. Watermarking, digital signatures, and blockchain technology can all play a role in establishing digital provenance, providing a tamper-proof record of a work's history. However, the effectiveness of these technologies depends on widespread adoption and interoperability. We need to develop open standards that allow different platforms and systems to communicate and exchange provenance information seamlessly, creating a unified ecosystem of trust and accountability.

Furthermore, the legal framework surrounding attribution needs to adapt to the challenges posed by new technologies and creative practices. Current copyright laws often struggle to address the complexities of digital authorship, particularly in cases involving collaborative works, algorithmically generated content, and derivative works. Legislators and policymakers need to work together to update existing laws and create new regulations that provide clear guidance on attribution in these emerging areas. This may involve clarifying the definition of authorship in the digital context, establishing clear rules for attributing the contributions of algorithms and other technologies, and developing mechanisms for resolving disputes over authorship in collaborative projects. The goal should be to create a legal framework that is flexible enough to adapt to future technological advancements, while still protecting the rights of authors and promoting innovation.

As we look to the future, it's important to recognize that attribution is not just a technical or legal problem; it's also a social and cultural one. Attribution is about recognizing and valuing the contributions of creators, fostering a culture of respect and appreciation for intellectual property. This requires educating the public about the importance of attribution, promoting ethical practices in content creation and distribution, and celebrating the creativity and innovation that drive our society forward. It also requires fostering a sense of responsibility among users of digital content, encouraging them to respect the rights of authors and to properly attribute their work when using or sharing it. Only by fostering a culture of attribution can we ensure that creators receive the recognition and rewards they deserve, and that our creative ecosystems continue to thrive.

7.2 Complex Collaboration Scenarios

As we move deeper into the digital age, collaborative projects are becoming increasingly common. These collaborations present unique challenges when it comes to assigning proper attribution. Complex collaboration scenarios demand a nuanced approach to applying attribution bounds. We must remember that these are not simply extensions of single-author attribution, but entirely new beasts to tackle. Consider a musical composition involving multiple songwriters, producers, and instrumentalists. Each individual contributes uniquely to the final product, however, the level of contribution can vary greatly. How do we fairly apportion credit when one songwriter provides the core melody, another the lyrics, and a third the harmonic structure? Or even a complex open source project, which sometimes involve many people for a large amount of time; here's where attribution might be even more complex.

One strategy is to employ a weighted attribution model, where each contributor receives a score based on the significance of their input. This scoring can be determined through a combination of self-reporting, peer assessment, and objective metrics, such as the number of lines of code contributed or the amount of time spent on a task. To ensure fairness, it is important to establish clear guidelines and criteria for assessing contributions from the outset of the project. This could involve creating a formal agreement that outlines the roles and responsibilities of each participant and specifies how attribution will be determined. For example, a project agreement might state that the lead designer will receive 40% of the attribution, while the other designers split the remaining 60% based on their individual contributions. Furthermore, consider different forms of collaboration. Some projects involve simultaneous contributions, while others are sequential, with one contributor building upon the work of another. The timing and nature of contributions can significantly impact their relative importance. In sequential collaborations, it may be appropriate to assign a higher attribution weight to the initial contributor, as their work forms the foundation for subsequent contributions. However, if the subsequent contributor significantly enhances or transforms the original work, they may also warrant a substantial portion of the attribution.

Consider the challenge of fairly attributing credit in projects involving both human and computer elements. It is also important to account for the nature of the contributions. Some contributions may be easily quantifiable, such as the number of illustrations created for a book or the amount of data collected for a research study. Other contributions may be more qualitative and difficult to measure, such as the creative direction provided by a project leader or the problem-solving skills demonstrated by a team member. In these cases, it may be necessary to rely on subjective assessments and expert opinions to determine the appropriate level of attribution. When multiple parties are involved, it's crucial to foster transparency and open communication.

When using statistical bounds in collaborative works, it's important to recognize that dependencies exist between the contributions of different authors. For instance, one author's contributions might heavily influence the direction or scope of another author's work. Failing to account for these dependencies can lead to inaccurate or unfair attribution. One way to address this issue is to use techniques from causal inference to model the relationships between different contributions. This can help to disentangle the direct and indirect effects of each author's work and to determine the extent to which one author's contributions depended on those of another. It's also important to consider the possibility of free-riding, where one author benefits from the contributions of others without making a substantial contribution themselves. If free-riding is suspected, it may be necessary to adjust the attribution weights accordingly to ensure fairness.

Now, let's consider the role of information theoretic bounds in complex collaborations. The concept of mutual information can be particularly useful in quantifying the degree of dependency between different authors' contributions. By measuring the amount of information that one author's work reveals about another author's work, we can gain insights into the extent to which their contributions are intertwined. For example, if two authors are working on related aspects of a project, their contributions are likely to have a high degree of mutual information. Conversely, if their contributions are largely independent, the mutual information will be low. The channel capacity concept can also be applied to collaborative scenarios to establish bounds on the amount of information that can be extracted from a collaborative work without violating attribution principles. This is particularly relevant in cases where one author is building upon the work of another, as it can help to determine the extent to which the derivative work is attributable to the original author. It is essential to clearly define the scope of the collaboration and to establish protocols for managing intellectual property rights.

Beyond these quantitative approaches, the social and ethical dimensions of collaboration should not be overlooked. Discussions about intellectual contribution can be emotional, so a good approach is to have clear and transparent communication. By proactively addressing potential attribution issues and engaging in open dialogue, collaborative teams can foster a culture of trust and respect, leading to more equitable and satisfying outcomes. Furthermore, the attribution process should be flexible and adaptable, allowing for adjustments as the project evolves and new information emerges. This can be achieved through regular check-ins, feedback sessions, and transparent decision-making processes. In conclusion, navigating complex collaboration scenarios requires a multifaceted approach that considers both technical and social factors. By combining rigorous analytical techniques with thoughtful communication and ethical considerations, we can create attribution frameworks that are fair, accurate, and promote a healthy collaborative environment.

7.3 Ethical Considerations

Attribution, while seemingly technical, is deeply intertwined with ethical considerations. The frameworks we develop to safeguard authors' production have far-reaching implications, touching upon fairness, bias, transparency, and the very definition of authorship itself. As these frameworks become more sophisticated, particularly with increased reliance on statistical and data-driven approaches, it's imperative to examine their ethical dimensions and ensure they align with societal values and principles of justice. Ignoring these aspects risks creating systems that, despite their technical prowess, perpetuate existing inequalities or introduce new forms of harm.

One of the most pressing ethical concerns revolves around bias in attribution models. Statistical attribution methods, for instance, are trained on data, and if that data reflects existing biases in the authorship landscape – such as underrepresentation of certain demographic groups or fields of study – the resulting models will inevitably amplify these biases. Consider a scenario where a model is designed to identify contributions to scientific publications. If the training data disproportionately features authors from prestigious institutions or particular geographic regions, the model may unfairly favor these individuals when assessing contributions to new, unseen publications. This can lead to marginalized authors being overlooked or undervalued, reinforcing existing inequalities in academic recognition and career advancement. Addressing this requires careful attention to data collection and preprocessing techniques, including strategies for identifying and mitigating biases in the training data. Furthermore, we must critically evaluate the model's outputs, looking for evidence of disparate impact across different groups and implementing fairness-aware algorithms that explicitly account for these differences. This also can happen in artistic expressions, where some styles may be given more merit than others.

Transparency and explainability are equally crucial. Attribution models, especially those based on complex statistical methods, can often be opaque "black boxes." It becomes challenging to understand why a particular attribution decision was made, making it difficult for authors to contest or challenge unfair outcomes. This lack of transparency can erode trust in the system and undermine its legitimacy. Imagine a situation where an attribution model is used to determine royalty payments for a collaborative musical work. If the model assigns a significantly smaller share of royalties to one of the collaborators, but the reasons for this decision are unclear, the affected author may feel unfairly treated and unable to seek redress. To address this, we need to prioritize the development of interpretable attribution models. This might involve using techniques like feature importance analysis to identify the factors that most heavily influence the model's decisions. Additionally, we can provide authors with clear and concise explanations of the attribution process, outlining the data used, the algorithms employed, and the rationale behind the final outcome. This would foster greater understanding and accountability, enabling authors to meaningfully engage with the attribution system and challenge decisions they believe are unjust.

Fairness extends beyond the individual author to encompass the broader community of creators. Attribution frameworks should not inadvertently stifle creativity or innovation by excessively restricting the use of existing works. Striking a balance between protecting authors' rights and promoting the free flow of information is essential. Overly stringent attribution requirements could discourage derivative works, remixes, and other forms of creative expression that build upon existing ideas. Conversely, lax attribution standards could lead to widespread plagiarism and the erosion of incentives for original work. A good example of this can be found on platforms that allow users to upload and remix content, in cases in which creators may feel discouraged to provide their work.

The definition of authorship itself is being challenged by the rise of collaborative creation and the increasing role of technology. Consider a situation where several researchers contribute to a scientific paper, and a sophisticated software tool is used to analyze the data and generate key findings. Determining the appropriate attribution for each contributor, including the software developers and the researchers who used the tool, becomes a complex ethical question. Should the software be considered an author, or should its contribution be attributed to the developers who created it? How should the researchers' intellectual input be weighed against the tool's contribution? There are no easy answers to these questions, and the ethical considerations will likely vary depending on the specific context and the nature of the contributions involved.

Furthermore, the application of attribution bounds in specific domains, such as scientific research, journalism, and artistic creation, raises unique ethical considerations. In scientific research, accurate and transparent attribution is paramount for maintaining the integrity of the scientific record and ensuring that researchers receive appropriate credit for their contributions. Misattribution or plagiarism can have serious consequences, including damage to reputation, loss of funding, and even retraction of publications. In journalism, attribution is crucial for maintaining credibility and avoiding accusations of bias or fabrication. Journalists must accurately attribute their sources and avoid presenting information as their own that was obtained from others. In artistic creation, attribution is often intertwined with issues of copyright and intellectual property. Artists have a right to control the use of their work and to receive credit for their creations. However, fair use principles allow for certain uses of copyrighted material without permission, such as parody, criticism, and education.

Enforcement of attribution bounds also raises ethical challenges. Implementing systems to monitor and detect violations of attribution requires careful consideration of privacy and freedom of expression. Overly intrusive monitoring systems could chill creative expression and stifle innovation. It's important to strike a balance between protecting authors' rights and safeguarding individual liberties. Suppose that automated systems are deployed to scan digital content for instances of plagiarism or unauthorized use of copyrighted material. These systems must be designed to respect privacy and avoid false positives, which could unfairly accuse innocent creators of wrongdoing. Furthermore, the process for investigating and resolving alleged violations of attribution should be fair and transparent, providing individuals with an opportunity to present their case and challenge the evidence against them.

Finally, we must acknowledge the global dimensions of ethical considerations. Attribution norms and practices can vary significantly across different cultures and legal systems. What is considered acceptable attribution in one country may be viewed as unethical or even illegal in another. In a globalized world, where digital content can easily cross borders, it's essential to develop attribution frameworks that are sensitive to cultural differences and promote international cooperation. This might involve establishing international agreements on attribution standards and creating mechanisms for resolving cross-border disputes.

In conclusion, the ethical considerations surrounding attribution are multifaceted and evolving. As we develop and deploy more sophisticated attribution frameworks, it's crucial to prioritize fairness, transparency, and respect for authors' rights. This requires addressing bias in attribution models, promoting explainability, striking a balance between protecting authors and fostering creativity, and being mindful of cultural differences and global implications. By carefully considering these ethical dimensions, we can ensure that attribution frameworks serve to promote justice, equity, and the flourishing of creative expression in the digital age.

www.ingramcontent.com/pod-product-compliance
Lightning Source LLC
LaVergne TN
LVHW022226200926
848481LV00006B/2146
* 9 7 9 8 3 4 9 5 4 4 9 9 6 *